HELICOPTER FIGHTERS

Andy Lightbody • Joe Poyer

Beekman House

Louis Weber, C.E.O.
Publications International, Ltd.
7373 North Cicero Avenue
Lincolnwood, Illinois 60646

Permission is never granted for commercial purposes.

Manufactured in Yugoslavia.

h g f e d c b a

ISBN 0-517-68762-3

This edition published by Beekman House. Distributed by Crown Publishers, Inc., 225 Park Avenue South, New York, New York 10003

Library of Congress Catalog Card Number: 89-63616

Contributing writers:

Andy Lightbody is coauthor of *The Illustrated History of Tanks*. He is also Editorial Director for *International Defense & Aerospace Magazine* and is the Military/Aerospace Editor for CBS Radio. Mr. Lightbody's articles appear frequently in the national and military trade press.

Joe Poyer, noted military affairs journalist and novelist, is coauthor of *The Illustrated History of Tanks*. He contributes regularly to numerous military publications, including *International Defense Images* and *International Combat Arms*.

Front cover: *French Panther 365*. **Back cover:** *American AH-64 Apache (top), American 530MG Defender (bottom)*.

Contents

Introduction:
On the Fighting Front

At 20,000 feet, the ground below is a collage of brown and green. At 500 feet, the land becomes a smear punctuated by missiles trailing wisps of smoke that reach up to strike the helicopter from the sky. On this eighth day of the war, mist hangs in the overcast sky that blankets much of central Europe. Those misty trails—tentacles of fog—are dangerous because they can conceal enemy fixed wing aircraft and helicopters.

The helicopter pilot makes a small course adjustment to bring his craft in behind the enemy armored formation. The weapons operator has his eyes glued to the sensor screens. The pilot twists his head like a World War I fighter pilot, searching the sky above and behind him.

Of the eight remaining AH-64A Apache helicopters in the squadron, only three were immediately flyable. They had been scrambled less than 20 minutes ago. A Soviet armored battalion was moving fast along a country road to flank a task force of the Army's 2nd Armored Cavalry Regiment that had taken a West German village only that morning. The village's value lay in the crossroads that it straddled. The Apaches were to disrupt and stop the Soviet column's movement in hopes of increasing its vulnerability to a strike by a battery of three Multiple Rocket Launchers located some 12 kilometers distant.

"Arming now," the weapons operator tells the pilot over the intercom.

On the pilot's display screen, the TOW II missile icon glows red. The pilot glances through the canopy at the other two helicopters in the strike force keeping station off his starboard side. He flexes his hand in the agreed upon signal. They dare not use their radios; Soviet jamming is fierce, and the Soviet's counter electronics warfare people would pick up the helicopters' radio signals instantly and warn the tank column.

The three helicopters slow and begin to lose altitude as they approach the forested ridge that overlooks the river valley. The scouting Apache had reported that the Soviet armor was moving in three columns: one on either side of the narrow valley and the third up the middle along the river. That meant the Apaches would receive the maximum fire from all three columns no matter how they approached.

The weapons operator keys his intercom. "Alpha 2, this is Hotel 1."

"Hotel 1, Alpha 2. We are hot. Go."

The weapons operator interprets this to mean that the Rangers—Alpha 2—were in position and ready to illuminate the target tanks with their laser designators.

"Alpha 2, Hotel 1. Light 'em up."

The AH-64A Apache's agility is one of its greatest assets against enemy armor.

The weapons operator signals the other two helicopters to make certain they had heard the exchange, and then three Hellfire missiles launch together. The missiles veer sharply skyward, then plunge over the ridge and down into the valley.

Without waiting, the pilot lifts the helicopter until it is standing on the ridge, the rocky crest only inches below the landing gear. The fire-and-forget Hellfire missiles pick up the laser-illuminated targets. The missiles' sensors steer the missiles directly toward the first and last tanks in the column. Both tanks burn fiercely. The third missile is nowhere to be seen.

The three weapons operators look at their instrument panels again and key in the TOW missile controllers. One after another they fire as targets come on line. The hair-thin control wires spin off their reels, following the missiles toward the tanks. For 10 dangerous seconds, the helicopters are exposed to the return fire of the heavily armed tank column. The weapons operators seek to keep their sights centered on their targets, struggling to overcome the aircraft's vibrations, the wind currents sweeping up the ridge, and the movements of the tanks themselves.

Ten seconds is long enough for the Soviet tankers to overcome their astonishment at the sudden destruction of two of their tanks, and they open fire. The Soviet tanks—T-72 Main Battle Tanks—are armed with 120 millimeter smoothbore guns and 12.7mm machine guns. The first 120mm round screams past, followed by a hail of copper-jacketed lead that rattles against the fuselage and canopy. The pilot swears, even as the TOW missiles strike. As the lead tank in the main column slews out of line, the weapons operator relinquishes control of the aircraft. The pilot turns away quickly, dropping back down behind the screening trees and heading for home.

"Hotel 1, Alpha 2. Good shooting. Five down."

As that acknowledgement rings through the radio waves, the first Multiple Rocket Launcher warheads burst over the valley, unleashing their deadly cargo of antitank mines.

The above scenario gives an idea of the role the modern fighting helicopter would have in the event of a war between NATO forces and Warsaw Pact forces.

Opposite: *This AH-64A, equipped with four auxiliary fuel tanks, can hold enough fuel to fly itself across the Atlantic.* **Above:** *The Apache's ability to carry either Hellfire or TOW missiles makes it a powerful anti-armor threat.* **Left:** *The AH-64A's 30mm chain gun fires rounds that can penetrate the armor of most main battle tanks.*

Development of the Attack Helicopter

The military history of the modern helicopter in the United States began in the last year of World War II with Igor Sikorsky and his R-4 helicopter. The R-4 and its successor, the R-6, saw service primarily in the China-Burma-India theater; it performed in the search and rescue and medevac roles. These roles continued during the Korean War, but the first experiments—largely unauthorized—toward arming the aircraft were conducted by helicopter crews. Hand grenades, carbines, shotguns, and even submachine guns were used to clear landing zones for search and rescue craft and during the first experiments with assault landings.

But it was not until the Vietnam War that a clear need was perceived for the armed helicopter. As early as 1962, attempts had been made to fly in troops to envelop enemy forces. But the enemy soon became more sophisticated in these encounters, and landing zones were quickly brought under attack. The toll of men and helicopters rose rapidly.

Machine guns and free-flight rockets were mounted on troop transports, but transports did not have the maneuverability to do the job properly. Aside from blanketing the immediate landing zone with fire from door-mounted machine guns, the helicopter crew was busy landing the craft and getting their passengers out. The crew could not do the total job very effectively.

What was needed was a dedicated gunship, that is, a helicopter whose only task was to escort troop-carrying helicopters, clear the landing zone before the transports landed, and then orbit the landing zone to suppress enemy fire. The first such gunship was the UH-1 Huey. It was armed with two fixed, forward firing M60 machine guns. Although the Huey did yeoman work, its range, weapons payload, and speed were limited. In a bid to improve the Huey's performance, the Bell Helicopter Company redesigned the standard Huey with a more powerful engine and narrower airframe. The resulting HueyCobra was a great deal faster and more maneuverable. It also carried heavier armament

Opposite: *These UH-1H Hueys belong to the U.S. Army's 24th Composite Squadron.* **Above:** *The UH-1 Huey received its baptism of fire in South Vietnam as a troop carrier and medevac chopper.* **Left:** *Although the UH-1 Huey is a multirole helicopter, it is first and foremost a medevac helicopter.*

in the form of a 7.62mm NATO minigun, a 40mm grenade launcher, and 76 2.75-inch rockets. HueyCobras could also carry additional minigun pods or even a 20mm cannon.

In the years following the Vietnam War, the use and function of the attack helicopter became a major topic in military and congressional services. The Marine Corps significantly up-rated their HueyCobras with sturdier air frames and heavier weaponry. This became the present AH-1W SuperCobra armed with TOW II missiles, which can destroy virtually any main battle tank in anyone's inventory. The Army developed the AH-64A Apache, a helicopter dedicated to tank-busting. Testing has shown the

Apache will also be viable in the anti-air role. The Army also developed the UH-60 Black Hawk, which can serve in the dual roles of general purpose utility helicopter, replacing the UH-1 Huey, and combat helicopter when armed with a variety of weapons.

The variety of helicopters available to military services illustrates the many roles of today's helicopter fighters. These aircraft can serve in combat roles from ground attack against troop convoys and antitank assault to fighting other helicopters and fixed wing aircraft.

Helicopter Weaponry

The helicopter has become an indispensable weapon on the modern battlefield. Modern tacticians were quick to see the value of the helicopter as a weapons platform. The first two military helicopters to see regular service, the German FA 223 and the Flettner FL 282, were armed with a machine gun and depth charges, respectively.

The concept of the helicopter as a gun platform was studied extensively after World War II at Fort Rucker, Alabama. The objective was to use the helicopter to suppress enemy ground fire during assault operations. Three weapon systems were developed that formed the basis of all modern helicopter weapon systems in use today.

The first weapon system developed was the XM-6 Quad—four M60 7.62mm NATO machine guns, two mounted on either side of the helicopter. The guns responded directly to a control system that allowed the pilot to aim and fire from the cockpit. The second weapon system developed was the 40mm grenade launcher, which enabled helicopter pilots to lay down a barrage of shrapnel to clear a landing zone. The third system was the adaptation of the French S-11 air-to-ground missile for helicopter use.

While these weapon developments were taking place, General Electric was reviving and modifying a gun system that had been developed at the beginning of the century. During the Civil War, a multiple-barrel weapon called the Gatling gun had been developed. It was manufactured by Colt Firearms and was improved during the 1870s and 1880s. The Gatling gun had a hand crank that turned multiple barrels past a fixed breech, developing an extremely high rate of fire. By the turn of the century, the U.S. Navy had modified the Gatling gun by replacing the hand crank with an electric motor. Rates of fire exceeding 1,000 rounds per minute were attained. These electrically driven Gatling guns were mounted on some naval vessels before the true machine gun became available.

General Electric updated the design and renamed it the minigun. The new design attained rates of fire of up to 3,000 rounds per minute. At last, the helicopter pilot had a weapon with which he could efficiently cover a landing zone. The first miniguns to be used were mounted in AH-1 HueyCobra gunships in 1966.

The development of the minigun led to the next step, the chain gun. Hughes Aircraft, now McDonnell Douglas Helicopter Company, developed a rapid-firing cannon. Ammunition was fed via a chain very much like a bicycle chain. The chain gun can fire 25mm and 30mm explosive-tip or armor-piercing bullets made of titanium or depleted uranium (a nonradioactive and very dense and heavy material). This ammunition can penetrate the armor of any tank in service today.

Further experimentation led to arming helicopters with rockets and missiles. The first such weapon to be adapted to the helicopter was the 2.75-inch free-flight rocket (FFR). This rocket was developed late in World War II for fixed wing fighter and attack aircraft. The French pioneered the helicopter-borne rocket during the early 1950s in Vietnam; they used 68mm FFRs. Free-flight rockets are mounted either individually in racks or in pods or boxes from which they can be fired singly or in waves. But despite the rocket's effectiveness, it was still unguided, and the pilot depended on a shotgun effect to make them effective.

The French Army developed two small guided missiles, the SS-10 and SS-11. Commands transmitted to the missile's guidance system over wires trailing behind it guided the missile to its target. During fighting in Algeria in the 1950s, the French developed a technique for firing these missiles from helicopters. The technique was called Manual Command, Line of Sight and improved the accuracy of missiles fired from a helicopter. However, the weapons operator had to actively steer the fast-moving missile to the target with a joystick. Thus the helicopter had to remain in view until the missile hit its target, exposing the helicopter to counter fire. The helicopter's vibrations and the movement of the target itself made it difficult to accurately steer the missile.

The next step was to design a missile guidance system that automated the flight steering mechanism. A Semiactive Command, Line of Sight system was developed and applied to the TOW (tube-launched, optically tracked, wire-guided) missile. In this system, a flare burns on the missile's tail after it has been launched. The weapons operator keeps his gun sight centered on the target. A sensor in the weapons operator's guidance unit measures the distance in angle between the flare and the target as seen in the sight. Signals are then sent to the missile's steering system. This solved the problem of helicopter vibrations but did nothing for the exposure of the helicopter to enemy fire.

A third-generation guidance system called Lock On After Launch (LOAL) was developed to eliminate this exposure problem. A LOAL-equipped missile is usually launched into a high trajectory path while a target designator illuminates the target with a laser, infrared beam, or radar beam. The guidance system is in the missile's nose, and it must see, or "acquire," the illumination. Once the guidance system sees the illumination, the sensors feed information to the missile's steering system, which directs the missile to the target.

The LOAL system enabled the helicopter pilot or weapons operator to either launch missiles from behind cover or launch missiles and quickly leave the area before the enemy could react. These missiles are known as fire-and-forget missiles since they allow the attacking helicopter to leave an area after firing. But the LOAL system requires that another helicopter or ground personnel designate (illuminate) the target, and the designator may be exposed to enemy fire.

An example of the LOAL system is the French-designed Exocet missile, which uses an active radar system to home in on its

target. Although the active radar does provide a warning to its victim, the active homing radar system does not turn on until the beginning of the terminal phase of the missile's flight, giving the enemy little time to react. The British Navy in the Falkland Islands in 1982 and the United States Navy in the Persian Gulf in 1987 discovered this fact to their dismay. Another example of the LOAL system is the British-designed Sea Skua missile. It functions in much the same way as the Exocet and achieved a great deal of success against Argentinean ships during the Falkland Islands War. Another type of fire-and-forget missile is the passive infrared system used in the Norwegian-designed Penguin air-to-surface antiship missile. This system is particularly well-suited for use at sea. While in flight, the missile searches until it finds a large heat source. Against the cold ocean, any large ship is an excellent heat source. The missile's sensors then direct the missile toward the warmest part of the target.

The next generation of missile guidance systems will use a built-in guidance system that will make the missile entirely independent after launch. This type of system will use a pattern recognition program. In effect, the missile's guidance system will search until it finds a target it recognizes. An internal computer will assess the shape, texture, and outline; decide whether the target is a Soviet T-80, an American M-1A1 Abrams, or a British Challenger; and act accordingly.

Finally, a new approach to helicopter-launched missiles is found in the hypervelocity missile. The guidance system is contained in the missile, which is powered by a rocket motor. The missile travels at 5,000 feet per second and strikes its target with 258,703 pounds per foot per second of energy. The helicopter version will launch fléchettes—small arrows—while in flight.

Opposite: This UH-1D Huey is equipped with the Army's Mk 56 mine dispenser system. **Above:** *A .50 caliber machine gun and a powerful searchlight are practically standard equipment on Hueys.*

A new area of helicopter weaponry involves air-to-air missiles and guns. Because of their ability to fly low and slow, helicopters are extremely hard for fixed wing aircraft to shoot down. Until the war between Iran and Iraq, there had not been any need to equip helicopters with air-to-air weaponry. But now even Third World nations include sizable helicopter forces. The air-to-air weapons used by fixed wing aircraft, particularly missiles that fly at less than Mach 1 speed and are highly maneuverable, work well against helicopters. But there are various other weapons that seem well-suited to helicopters.

The Stinger missile has been tested extensively. This missile was originally developed to allow infantry troops to defend themselves against low-flying attack aircraft, and it proved its worth in Afghanistan. For tank busting, the TOW missile and the West German-designed HOT missile have been installed in helicopters, most notably the AH-1 HueyCobra and SeaCobra versions. But tests have shown that HOT and TOW missiles are also well-suited for the anti-air role. The Marines' AH-1W SuperCobra carries the AIM-9L Sidewinder air-to-air missile to defend amphibious landing zones from attack by fixed wing aircraft.

Tests have shown that the lighter caliber miniguns firing 7.62mm NATO rounds are of limited usefulness against such helicopters as the Soviet Mi-24 Hind because of its heavy armor plating. But the McDonnell Douglas chain gun, firing 25mm or 30mm armor-piercing rounds such as the M789 bullet at 625 rounds per minute, makes the helicopter a deadly adversary.

The Helicopter Fighter Today

Since the end of the Vietnam War there have been four major conflicts that involved the helicopter to a large extent: the Soviet invasion of Afghanistan, the war between Iran and Iraq, the United States invasion of Grenada, and the Falkland Islands War between Argentina and Great Britain. Each of these engagements has taught lessons about the use of helicopters in combat situations.

The Soviet experience with helicopters in Afghanistan was similar to that of the United States in Vietnam. Helicopters are vulnerable to ground fire, even small arms fire. The Soviets armored their fighting as well as their transport helicopters against shot up to 12.7mm. While this did not make attack helicopters invulnerable to ground fire, the armor did offer significant protection to crew and craft. As a result, Soviet rotary wing losses were lower, on a percentage basis, than American rotary wing losses in Vietnam.

The situation in Afghanistan remained this way until 1985. In that year, the United States and Great Britain began to supply the Afghan resistance fighters with portable, shoulder-launched antiaircraft missiles. The American Stinger missile and the British Blowpipe missile quickly turned the tables. By early 1989, when they withdrew their forces from Afghanistan, the Soviets had lost nearly 1,000 aircraft, 80 percent of which were helicopters. The fast, heavily armored Soviet Mi-24 Hind accounted for 200 of the helicopter losses. Nearly 60 percent of all Soviet aircraft combat losses in Afghanistan are credited to the Stinger or the less frequently used Blowpipe.

Although these one-man antiaircraft missiles seemed to redress the imbalance between combat helicopters and the ground soldier, Soviet helicopter pilots developed several techniques to decrease vulnerability. Flare dispensers were mounted on all combat helicopters to decoy the approaching missile away from the aircraft's engine exhausts. Flights were scheduled at higher altitudes and landings and takeoffs were considerably more precipitous. The tactics were successful enough that the toll of helicopters dropped in the last 18 months of the war.

In the war between Iran and Iraq during the 1980s, little is known yet about actual combat operations. Both nations took particular pains to keep neutral, or even friendly, observers away from the battlefields. By and large, the only journalists allowed to cover the war were their own citizens, and their goal was propaganda, not factual reporting.

Nevertheless, we know that the helicopter played a significant role on both sides. The battlefield terrain was sparsely vegetated and mostly low, coastal plain and desert. There were few hills or natural obstacles to provide cover. Armed helicopters were used to shoot down troop-carrying helicopters, and both sides used armed helicopters in the air-to-air combat role to shoot one another down. But, except for proving the viability of air-to-air helicopter combat, few other details have surfaced.

The United States' invasion of Grenada in 1983, known as Operation Urgent Fury, was far more instructive than the Iran-Iraq conflict despite its short-lived nature. A total of 107 helicopters were used in amphibious operations and in the utility role.

Continued on page 18

Opposite: An antitank version of the French Ecureuil. Above: This SH-60B Seahawk is searching for a submarine with a Magnetic Anomaly Detector. Left: The UH-60A Black Hawk can carry a fully equipped 11-man infantry squad.

Above: *This French SA 365 Panther carries the GIAT 20mm cannon.* **Right:** *The large circular radar antenna housing for the Seahawk's APS-124 search radar can clearly be seen here.*

Above: *This French Ecureuil, a fast and maneuverable helicopter, is armed with twin launchers for TOW missiles.*
Left: *The French Panther can carry a variety of weapons, including launchers capable of firing 12 68mm rockets.*

Above, left: *When at sea, the SH-60B Seahawk is attached to Oliver Hazard Perry-class destroyers in the LAMPS III role. The remainder of the Navy's Seahawks operate from shore bases.* **Above, right:** *The Sensor Operator of the SH-60B Seahawk operates the radar, sonar, magnetic anomaly detector, and electronic support measures equipment.*

Continued from page 14

The Marine Corps HMM-261 Squadron (New River, North Carolina) used 22 helicopters to ferry in the assault teams and their supplies. Marine Corps SeaCobras were used in the gunship role but were particularly vulnerable to Soviet-supplied antiaircraft weaponry. Two HueyCobras were shot down while supporting Army units during the breakout from Port Salinas, and three of the four crew members were killed. The surviving crew member suffered extensive injuries. One UH-60 Black Hawk was shot down, and five others were extensively damaged. A CH-46E Sea Knight was shot down by ground fire and had to be destroyed by an AC-130 gunship.

Operation Urgent Fury raised the question of the survivability of the helicopter on the modern battlefield. The Grenadian forces and their Cuban allies did not possess any particularly sophisticated antiaircraft weaponry. The only truly antiaircraft weapons they had were a few ZSU-23 antiaircraft guns, which are double-barreled but are manually aimed and fire 23mm projectiles.

But if the invasion of Grenada raised red flags, British operations during the Falkland Islands War proved the helicopter's worth. Stories are numerous—and legendary—concerning the heroism and sacrifice of British helicopter pilots. Loads of troops two and three times the normal number were transported in darkness at less than tree-top height to positions that outflanked the Argentinean forces. Helicopters plucked commando teams off glaciers in the midst of raging blizzards. Two Royal Navy Lynx helicopters are credited with sinking at least two Argentinean ships with the new, *untested* Sea Skua missile. A Wasp helicopter damaged the submarine *Santa Fe* with depth charges.

Above: *An artist's rendering of one idea for a new light multirole helicopter for the U.S. Army.*

The Helicopter Fighter's Future

Military experience with the helicopter since 1944 has assured it a place in the arsenals of all major, and most minor, powers. Certainly the Soviets think so. They have two new major helicopter designs in the final testing stages. In fact, deployment of both has been delayed to incorporate the lessons learned in Afghanistan.

The first is the fast, heavily armed Mi-28 Havoc, which will succeed the Mi-24 Hind. The other is the Ka-36 Hokum, the first helicopter in the world to be designed specifically for the air-to-air combat role. Both helicopters are discussed in detail in the Soviet section of this book's helicopter profiles.

Currently, the United States deploys more than 1,000 AH-64A Apaches to U.S. Army forces at home and abroad. Under development is a new helicopter that will serve in both the scouting and attack roles. Designated the LHX (Light Helicopter, Experimental), this all-new helicopter will make extensive use of composite materials and stealth technology to decrease its vulnerability to enemy ground and antiaircraft fire.

Another helicopter development waiting in the wings is the V-22 Osprey, which is a promising mix of helicopter and fixed wing attributes. Although not a combat helicopter, the Osprey has characteristics that may be seen on fighting helicopters of the future. This new composite aircraft has two large engines outboard on the wings. The engines rotate up to enable the aircraft to take off and land like a helicopter. While flying, the engines rotate down until parallel with the ground, enabling the Osprey to fly like a fixed wing aircraft. Since the Osprey can land like a helicopter on assault transports, freighters, or other warships, the Marine Corps is particularly interested in the Osprey to support amphibious landings. The Air Force is interested in using the Osprey for the search and rescue role and for special warfare air operations.

A European consortium has been trying for nearly 10 years without success to establish parameters and design specifications for a multinational combat helicopter. All the nations involved agree that such a helicopter is needed, but they cannot agree on the specifics. In the meantime, Italy has recently begun to deploy the highly capable Agusta 129 Mongoose, a helicopter dedicated to the antitank role and as capable as the United States' AH-64A Apache.

It is certain the helicopter will continue to prove more and more useful in the military role as technology improves the helicopter's flight characteristics and weapons capability.

BELL UH-1 IROQUOIS (HUEY)

Bell Model 204

There is perhaps no more successful helicopter ever designed and built for military or civilian use than the UH-1 Iroquois, better known as the Huey after its original U.S. military designation, HU-1. The Huey has been uprated far beyond its original capabilities and remains the most widely used utility helicopter in the United States armed forces.

The UH-1 Huey, the mainstay of American and Army of the Republic of Vietnam forces during the Vietnam War, first flew in 1956 as Bell Helicopter's Model 204. The Model 204 was originally designed as a light utility helicopter to meet the specifications of the United States Army's XH-40 program. The Huey entered military service as the HU-1A and went to Vietnam as an air ambulance in 1962.

The Huey was the first production helicopter to be equipped with a gas turbine engine. The original engine was a Lycoming T33 capable of developing 770 horsepower. The overall weight of the Huey in its A configuration was 5,800 pounds. As Lycoming engineers improved the T33 engine's performance until it was capable of developing 1,100 horsepower, Bell engineers were able to build an even larger airframe, the UH-1H. The UH-1H could carry up to 14 fully equipped troops or six stretcher casualties compared with the eight soldiers or three stretchers of the earlier UH-1.

The UH-1H (Bell civilian designation: Model 205) is powered by a T53-L-13 gas turbine engine. The Huey was the first U.S. military helicopter to have an engine mounted on top of and behind the cabin roof. This type of mounting eased the problems of gearing the main shaft and tail rotor and left the cargo and cockpit space clear of drive shafts and engine bulkheads. Five separate fuel tanks hold a total of 223 gallons of fuel.

The fuselage is of monocoque construction, covered in sheet metal. In monocoque construction, the skin covering the fuselage absorbs most of the stress, allowing use of a relatively light tube-steel framework. The pilot sits in the left-

Although helicopters had been used in the Korean War, the Vietnam War brought home to military planners the helicopter's versatility.

Above: *Lt. Commander William D. Martin, U.S. Navy, lands near a South Vietnamese outpost on the Bassac River after a mission against suspected Viet Cong positions.* **Opposite, top:** *Assault troops practice techniques for descending from a hovering Bell UH-1 Huey.* **Opposite, bottom:** *A UH-1 Huey lifts a Gamma Goat slung beneath its fuselage.*

hand seat, the copilot or weapons operator in the right. When configured as a troop carrier or gunship, the crew chief serves as door gunner. When configured as an ambulance, a medic is often carried in the main compartment.

The rotor system derives from the successful system developed by Bell and first used on the Bell H-13 (Model 47). The rotor blades themselves originally were extruded aluminum spars laminated together. These blades are now being replaced by stronger blades of glass fiber composite over a NOMEX honeycomb core construction. The trailing blade edge is also glass fiber. The leading edge has a polyurethane covering over a stainless steel sheath, which enables the blade to cut through unexpected obstructions like small tree branches when the aircraft is flying at low altitudes.

The UH-1H carries standard avionics equipment including UHF, FM, and VHF radios; an identification, friend or foe system; and various navigation aids, depending on what the buyer orders. Bell also offers an optional cargo hook, rescue hoist, and additional fuel tanks.

Since more than 7,000 UH-1s of various configurations have been purchased by more than a dozen nations, the Bell UH-1 has been armed with just about every type of weaponry that a helicopter of its weight and payload capacity can carry. Unless operating in a war zone, most Hueys on military service are unarmed. But if there can be said to be any standard armament for the Huey, it is probably three 7.62 NATO M60 machine guns, one mounted on each skid and one in a door mount operated by the crew chief. In addition, the Huey can carry various-sized containers of 2.75-inch free-flight rockets. The Huey may carry other weapons systems, including but not limited to 20 millimeter and 25mm cannons in pod mounts, 7.62mm NATO miniguns, .50 caliber machine guns, rocket launchers up to 3.2 inches, 40mm grenade launchers, various antitank missiles, various air-to-ground missiles, and for naval service, depth charges and Mark 44 and Mark 46 torpedoes.

A twin-engined version of the Huey, the UH-1N Iroquois, is powered by the Pratt & Whitney Canada T400-CP-400 Turbo "Twin Pac," which con-

Above: *The Huey was used extensively in Vietnam to transport assault troops to secure a landing zone.* **Opposite, top:** *Army helicopter crews, like this one in a UH-1 Huey armed with an M60D machine gun, practice constantly to keep in top form.* **Opposite, bottom:** *The crew chief of this UH-1B Huey, Sgt. Dennis Troxel, rides shotgun in support of the 4th Infantry Division in the northern highlands of Vietnam.*

sists of two PT6 turboshaft engines coupled to a single transmission. The UH-1N, which is flown by the United States Air Force, can be armed with two seven-tube launchers for 2.75-inch free-flight rockets and either two General Electric 7.62mm NATO miniguns or two 40mm grenade launchers.

The United States Army modified numerous UH-1Hs to the EH-1H configuration to provide a tactical battlefield electronic countermeasures capability for a project called Quick Fix I. The EH-1Hs were provided with a radar warning receiver, airborne communications interception equipment, chaff and flare dispensers, and an infrared jammer. The Army also converted 220 UH-1Hs to UH-1V medevac helicopters.

The famed Huey has been flying for U.S. military services since 1962 and will continue to do so well into the 21st century. They will continue to perform resupply, troop carrying, electronic warfare, medical evacuation, and mine dispersing operations as needed. Today's Huey is far more capable than the first UH-1As and UH-1Bs that saved so many lives in Vietnam. The Hueys of tomorrow will be even more capable after they are fitted with new composite blades, radar altimeters, infrared jammers and suppressors, new chaff and flare dispensers, and improved avionics and communications gear.

The Bell 204/205 model in civilian and military configurations has been built by Bell, by Agusta in Italy, and in Japan and Taiwan under license. No other aircraft has been built for military service in any country in such quantity since the end of World War II than the venerable Huey.

BELL UH-1H IROQUOIS (HUEY)

Main rotor
  diameter: 48 ft.
Tail rotor
  diameter: 8 ft., 6 in.
Length: 57 ft., 9.5 in.
Width: 9 ft., 6.5 in.
Height: 11 ft., 9.75 in.
Weight (maximum
  take-off): 9,500 lbs.
Cruising speed: 127 mph
Maximum
  altitude: 12,600 ft.
Range: 318 miles
Date of first
  flight: 1961

The Bell UH-1B Huey gave American and South Vietnamese troops close air support, day or night, during the Vietnam War.

Above: *Bell UH-1 Hueys.
have been built in greater
numbers, more than 7,000,
than any other military
aircraft since World War II.*
Right: *All U.S. military
helicopters are configured
first and foremost for medical
evacuation.*

Above: This UH-1B Huey mounts an M5 40mm grenade launcher. Up to 200 grenades per minute can be fired at ranges to 1,600 yards to clear landing zones and suppress enemy fire. **Left:** Members of the 20th Operations Squadron perform open-water exercises using a specially painted UH-1N.

Air mobile operations have become a standard military tactic. Helicopters, like these UH-1H Hueys, can airlift troops behind enemy lines before the enemy can react.

McDONNELL DOUGLAS 530M DEFENDER

McDonnell Douglas Model 500M

The wasp-like Defender resulted from the United States Army's Light Observation Helicopter (LOH) competition in the early 1960s. The roles allotted to the LOH at that time were medical evacuation, close support, photo reconnaissance, light transport, and observation. Of 12 companies entering the competition, only three—Bell, Fairchild Hiller, and Hughes—were selected to develop five prototypes each. Trials were carried out at Fort Rucker, Alabama, in 1963 and were completed on May 26, 1965. The Hughes entry was announced the winner.

Introduced as the OH-6A Cayuse, only 1,434 of the anticipated 4,000 light helicopters had been built by the time production ended in 1970. The OH-6A was extremely fast and agile as well as durable—one was shot down five times in South Vietnam and repaired each time—but far more costly to build than anticipated. The vast majority of the OH-6As were used in South Vietnam to support American and Army of the Republic of Vietnam forces. They were known there as "Loaches," derived from the acronym, LOH.

Hughes Helicopter—which became a subsidiary of McDonnell Douglas in 1984—continued to build the OH-6A under the designation Model 500 for civilian use as a corporate helicopter. To expand its market, Hughes developed an armed military model for export and sold it under the Model 500M designation. The Model 500M, which used the same Allison T63-A-5A turboshaft engine as the earlier OH-6A, was introduced in 1968. It has been extremely popular with smaller nations and is, or has been, in service in Colombia, Denmark, Mexico, the Philippines, and Spain. It has been built under license by RACA in Argentina, Kawasaki in Japan, and BredaNardi in Italy.

To keep the 500M current, Hughes developed the 500M Defender (500MD), which carried the Hughes B6M-71 TOW, a wire-guided missile. The

This McDonnell Douglas 530 Defender is armed with a .50 caliber machine gun pod and twin TOW antitank missile launchers.

Above: *The OH-6A Cayuse, the predecessor to the Defender, was a fast and agile helicopter used for scouting and as a light gunship in South Vietnam.*
Right: *The MD 530 Defender can be fitted with an amazing variety and weight of armor (left to right): 12-tube 2.75-inch rocket launcher, twin 7.62mm machine gun pod, .50 caliber machine gun pod, 7-tube 2.75-inch rocket launcher, and twin Stinger antiaircraft missile launcher.*

TOW missile had first seen action in Vietnam in 1972, when two UH-1B Hueys between them smashed 62 targets in one battle.

The original OH-6A was the first production light helicopter to use a gas turbine engine. The Allison T63-A-5A produced 317 horsepower, derated to 252 horsepower for takeoff and 215 horsepower for maximum cruising speed. The engine gave the small helicopter such extraordinary performance that it set 23 world records. The 530MD series, an up-rated version of the 500MD series, uses a more powerful 420 horsepower Allison 250-C-20B turboshaft engine.

The OH-6A Cayuse employed a four-bladed main rotor 26 feet 4 inches in diameter and a single, twin-bladed tail rotor mounted at the end of the tail boom. A vertical, down-pointing stabilizer helped offset engine torque. The helicopters in the 500/530 series can be differentiated from the original OH-6A by the five-bladed main rotor and the tail rotor mounted inside a T-shaped stabilizer.

Five basic variations are offered in the 500/530 series. The 500MD Scout Defender is the basic military version and is now in use in Kenya and by the South Korean Air Force. The Scout Defender carries a wide variety of armament, including 2.75-inch rockets, a 7.62mm NATO minigun, and a 40mm grenade launcher or a 7.62mm chain gun. The 500MD/TOW Defender is an antitank version of the Scout Defender and comes armed with four TOW air-to-ground missiles mounted in

two pods. The TOW Defender can be easily identified by the TOW pods on outriggers at the rear of the cabin and by the turret, which houses the TOW sight, slung under the nose. This version is used by South Korea, Kenya, and Israel. The 500MD/ASW Defender is equipped for antisubmarine work. It carries surface search radar, a towable magnetic anomaly detector, smoke marker launchers, shipboard haul down winch, and two Mark 44 or Mark 46 homing torpedoes. This version has been purchased by the Taiwan Navy. The 530MF Defender is an assault, support, and anti-armor helicopter, but it can also perform scouting, day/night surveillance, utility, and cargo-lift missions.

The 530MG Defender is the latest version to be offered in this well-tested series. It is powered by the Allison 250-C30 turboshaft engine producing 650 horsepower. The 530MG Defender can carry 2.75-inch rockets, TOW missiles, 7.62mm and .50 caliber machine guns, Stingers, and the 7.62mm McDonnell Douglas chain gun. Based on the larger, more powerful civilian MD 530F Lifter, the 530MG integrates much of the technology that will appear in the United States Army's Light Helicopter Experimental (LHX) program, which is designed to produce a new light, all-purpose helicopter by the mid-1990s. With further cuts in the United States military budget possible, it is conceivable that the 530 MG Defender could be substituted for the multibillion dollar LHX program.

More than 1,400 OH-6As were built and saw service in South Vietnam.

McDONNELL DOUGLAS 530MG DEFENDER

Main rotor diameter:	27 ft., 4 in.
Tail rotor diameter:	4 ft., 9 in.
Length:	25 ft.
Width:	6 ft., 4.75 in.
Height:	8 ft., 8 in.
Weight (maximum take-off):	3,000 lbs.
Cruising speed:	137 mph
Maximum altitude:	16,000 ft.
Range:	207 miles
Date of first flight:	1963

Top: The OH-6A Cayuse was intended as a light observation helicopter only, but in Vietnam it was soon turned into a gunship. **Bottom:** The Cayuse's ability to hide among the trees made it an excellent weapon against enemy armor and troop concentrations in Vietnam.

McDonnell Douglas has developed a special night fighter version of the 530 Defender called the "Nightfox." It carries a pod-mounded forward-looking infrared system for night vision and a 7.62mm chain gun.

The 530 Defender is an excellent anti-armor helicopter when carrying two twin TOW antitank missile launchers and the Hughes Aircraft M-65 TOW sight.

Top: *The 530 Defender's Allison gas turbine powerplant makes it fast and agile enough for ground-hugging missions against enemy armor.* **Bottom:** *The OH-6A Cayuse first flew in 1963; this photograph of an OH-6A test aircraft was taken in July 1968.*

BELL AH-1 HUEYCOBRA

Bell Model 209

To the untrained eye, the shorter and far more slender AH-1 HueyCobra looks nothing like its parent, the fat-bodied, lumbering UH-1 Huey. In 1965, Bell Helicopter began to develop a specific Huey variation to serve as an armed helicopter to escort slow, unarmed or lightly armed transports and medevac choppers. Today, the AH-1W SuperCobra is a "do anything, go anywhere" combat helicopter that can fly escort missions or bust tanks.

The HueyCobra first flew in September 1965; by March 1966, the United States Army had placed its first order. Basically, the new helicopter (Bell Model 209) retained the engine, transmission, and other major parts of the Model 205, but replaced the bulky fuselage with a new, thin-profile fuselage. Stub wings were added to ease the load on the main rotor and serve as attaching points for additional weapons. The narrow fuselage dictated a tandem cockpit seating arrangement; the pilot was placed behind and above the copilot/weapons operator.

A turret was mounted under the nose of the fuselage to carry miniguns, rapid firing cannons, or grenade launchers. These weapons were controlled by the copilot/weapons operator, who could slew them in wide arcs either side to side or up and down. When the copilot/weapons operator released the weapon controls, the turret resumed a locked fore and aft position. The copilot/weapons operator could also fly the helicopter from his station. The pilot was able to fire the nose turret weapons from his position but only when the turret was in the locked position. The pilot was responsible for firing the weapons mounted on the stub wings.

The HueyCobra has gone through a number of modifications since it first entered service. Initially, it was intended only as an interim system until the larger, more capable Lockheed AH-56 Cheyenne development was completed. But when the Cheyenne was canceled in 1972, Bell began to plan seriously for up-rated models.

The AH-1 HueyCobra's narrow profile and ability to carry a wide range of armament makes it a very effective combat aircraft.

Above: *AH-1 HueyCobra attack helicopters lined up on the apron during Operation Bright Star exercises in Egypt.* **Right:** *To increase the performance of the AH-1, a four-bladed main rotor was added to Marine Corps SeaCobras and renamed SuperCobras.*

The initial model designation of the HueyCobra was AH-1G. The AH-1G was powered by a Lycoming T53-L-13 turboshaft engine producing 1,100 horsepower. The United States Army acquired the majority of the AH-1Gs produced, but Israel and the Spanish Navy ordered six and eight respectively. The United States Marine Corps ordered a twin engine version, the AH-1J SeaCobra. Two Pratt & Whitney Canada T400-CP-400 twin turboshaft engines coupled to a single transmission provided 1,100 horsepower for the SeaCobra as well as the insurance of an extra engine for over-the-water emergencies.

Soon, however, the Army wanted an attack helicopter powerful enough to cope with the growing threat of Soviet and Warsaw Pact tanks. The B6M-71 TOW provided the Army with a guided missile potent enough to destroy any Soviet main battle tank. The wire guidance system gave the missile the required precision when fired from the relatively long range needed by a hovering helicopter. The first HueyCobra model to be fitted with the TOW was the AH-1Q, which was intended as an interim solution until the modernized HueyCobra, the AH-1S, could be developed.

The modernized versions of the HueyCobra were delivered in three phases. The first AH-1S, which entered Army service in March 1977, had a flat plate canopy instead of the earlier rounded panels, to reduce sun glint. It was also equipped with new, more extensive electronics and the up-rated Lycoming T53-L-703 1,800 horsepower turboshaft engine. The next phase was an up-gunned AH-1S equipped with a new universal turret able to mount either a 20 millimeter or 30mm gun. This version also had other modifications to improve the handling of weapons. The third phase was termed the "modernized" AH-1S.

Besides including the improvements of the first two phases, these HueyCobras carried new composite rotor blades, a new fire control system that included a laser range finder, an improved navigation system, and an infrared jammer. All versions of the AH-1S are capable of firing the TOW missile.

The most recent enhancement for the Huey-Cobra is the C-NiTE project, which provides the HueyCobra with the ability to kill tanks at night. The C-NITE sight uses the tank thermal imager developed for the M-1 Abrams Main Battle Tank and the TOW 2 system video thermal tracker from the Bradley Armored Fighting Vehicle. This new sight allows the HueyCobra to find and destroy tanks at night or in heavy fog or smoke conditions.

Other versions of the HueyCobra include the United States Marines' AH-1T SeaCobra and AH-1W SuperCobra. The AH-1T, which carries a more powerful Pratt & Whitney Canada T400-WV-402, is an up-rated version of the twin-engine AH-1J. The AH-1W SuperCobra "Whiskey," originally called the AH-1T+, is powered by twin General Electric T700-GE-401 turboshaft engines producing 3,250 horsepower. All AH-1T SeaCobras in the Marine Corps inventory have now been up-rated to the AH-1W configuration.

In keeping with the Marine Corps' self-definition as a "lean, mean fighting machine," the AH-1W can perform missions ranging from anti-armor to search and destroy and target acquisition. The AH-1W can carry a wide variety of armaments: a 20mm three-barrel M197 gun or up to eight Hellfire or TOW missiles and either 76 2.75-inch or 16 5-inch Zuni rockets or, for air-to-air combat, either two 20mm pods or two AIM-9L Sidewinder missiles.

An AH-1S HueyCobra over the Mohave Desert during Gallant Eagle training exercises.

BELL AH-1S HUEYCOBRA

Main rotor diameter:	·44 ft.
Tail rotor diameter:	8 ft., 6 in.
Length:	44 ft., 7 in.
Width:	3 ft., 3 in.
Height:	13 ft., 5 in.
Weight (maximum take-off):	10,000 lbs.
Cruising speed:	141 mph
Maximum altitude:	12,200 ft.
Range:	315 miles
Date of first flight:	1965

Opposite: As Marines storm ashore during an amphibious operation, a SeaCobra armed with an M197 20mm cannon and 2.75-inch rocket launchers hovers overhead. **This page, top:** AH-1 HueyCobras were developed during the Vietnam War to protect Huey transport helicopters. **This page, bottom:** During exercises at Fort Hood, Texas, an AH-1G HueyCobra swoops in to harass "enemy" armored forces.

The turret under the nose of this AH-1 HueyCobra can carry either two 7.62mm miniguns, two 40mm grenade launchers, or one of each.

Above: *This close-up of an AH-1 shows the old-style canopy, since replaced by flat glass plates to reduce glare.* **Right:** *The HueyCobra excels as a tank-buster.* **Opposite, top:** *The HueyCobra "Patricia Ann" flies patrol during the Vietnam War.* **Opposite, bottom:** *Although second to the newer AH-64A Apache, the HueyCobra is still a formidable weapon.*

SIKORSKY UH-60A BLACK HAWK/ SH-60B SEAHAWK

Sikorsky Model S-70

In the early 1970s, the United States Army identified a need for a more advanced utility helicopter than the UH-1 Huey that would perform a variety of roles into the next century. A proposal for a program called Utility Tactical Transport Aircraft System (UTTAS) was developed, and in 1972, two companies, Sikorsky and Boeing Vertol, were selected to supply prototypes. In late December 1976, the Army selected Sikorsky as the prime contractor; the first deliveries of the new UH-60A Black Hawk were made in 1978.

The Black Hawk is a traditionally designed helicopter with a single main rotor and a boom-mounted tail rotor. The main rotor can survive hits from .50 caliber or 23 millimeter armor-piercing shells. The rotor hub uses elastomeric bearings that do not need lubrication and require far less maintenance than traditional metal bearings. The blade tips are swept back 20 degrees, and the trailing edges have tabs to improve airflow. The blades are made of hollow titanium spars, NO-MEX honeycomb cores, graphite trailing edges, and glass fiber leading edges, and covered with glass fiber and epoxy skins. The leading edges are sheathed in titanium.

Two General Electric T700-700 turboshaft engines provide 1,543 horsepower each and drive a single transmission. The Black Hawk also carries a Solar 90-horsepower auxiliary power unit, a small gas turbine engine, for operations independent of ground support. The fuel system was designed to be crashworthy—that is, in most crashes the fuel is not expected to catch fire or explode. The fuselage is sufficiently armored to withstand hits from .30 caliber weapons, such as the AK-47 assault rifle and its derivatives. The Black Hawk can be armed with one or two side-mounted machine guns, Hellfire guided missiles,

The crews of UH-60A Black Hawks rotate from the United States to Honduras for 14-day periods in an effort to train troops under more realistic conditions.

Above: *The UH-60A Black Hawk can carry auxiliary fuel tanks and a variety of weapons on the External Store Support System wings.* **Opposite:** *The Navy version of the Black Hawk is the SH-60 Seahawk.*

2.75-inch rockets, and the M56 mine-dispersing system. The Black Hawk carries a crew of three, and the pilot's and copilot's seats are armored. The aircraft can also carry a full infantry squad (11 troops), but as many as 14 soldiers can be crammed into the main cabin in what Sikorsky denotes as "high-density seating." Eight of the seats can be replaced with racks for four stretchers. The Black Hawk is equipped with an external cargo hook with an 8,000-pound cargo capacity. Despite its capacity, the Black Hawk is small enough that one can be carried in a C-130 Hercules, two in a C-141 Starlifter, and six in a C-5 Galaxy transport aircraft.

Since its introduction in 1978, the UH-60A Black Hawk has undergone a number of modifications for specialized missions. The Army developed the EH-60A to carry Quick Fix IIB electronic countermeasures equipment for disrupting and monitoring enemy battlefield communications. The EH-60A can be identified by the four dipole antennae that project above and below the boom and the whip antennae attached beneath the fuselage.

The Air Force ordered a version of the UH-60A, known as the HH-60A Night Hawk, to be used as a combat rescue helicopter. The Night Hawk,

armed with 7.62mm NATO machine guns, can conduct rescue missions up to 287 miles distant, day or night, without an escort. The Air Force is also purchasing a second version of the UH-60A, known as the MH-60G Pave Hawk, which is an outgrowth of the interim Credible Hawk rescue helicopter program. The Pave Hawk is a Night Hawk that will be fitted with special instrumentation, including radar, electronic map displays, tactical air navigation systems, and .50 caliber machine guns.

The Marine Corps has purchased nine VH-60A Black Hawks to replace its VH-1N Hueys in the Executive Flight Detachment of Marine Helicopter Squadron 1, the unit that flies the President and other top administration officials.

The Navy has also purchased a variation of the S-70, designated the SH-60B Seahawk, for their Light Airborne Multipurpose System (LAMPS) Mark III program. The Navy's version differs from the Army's in having marinized gas turbine engines (specially constructed engines for operation in a humid, salty environment), chin pods, pylon mounts to hold either two Mark 44 or Mark 46 homing torpedoes or extra fuel tanks, magnetic anomaly equipment, a fourth crew space for the sensor operator, greater fuel capacity, rescue

Above: *The UH-60A Black Hawk can carry a fully equipped infantry squad.*

hoist, automatic blade-folding devices for the main and tail rotors, and a haul-down device for landing the helicopter on small ships in rough seas. The Seahawk can also refuel while hovering.

The Navy is deploying the Seahawk on all Oliver Hazard Perry-class frigates, Spruance-class and Aegis destroyers, and Ticonderoga-class cruisers, a total of 106 ships. The Seahawk is replacing the earlier LAMPS Mark I SH-2D Seasprites and will provide greater range, endurance,

and time available to track a target than the Seasprites.

Another Navy version of the Seahawk, the SH-60F, is being deployed as an antisubmarine warfare (ASW) helicopter to patrol the "inner zone" of an aircraft carrier battle group. Instead of LAMPS equipment, the SH-60F carries specialized ASW instrumentation, including dipping sonar and Mark 50 homing torpedoes. The Navy has also ordered a combat search and rescue version, the HH-60H, that can also support Navy SEAL and

UDT (Sea Air Land commandoes and Underwater Demolition Team) special forces.

The Seahawk has been so successful that it has carried out 97 percent of all assigned missions since it entered service. Seahawks are flown by the Royal Australian and Spanish navies. The Japanese Marine Self Defense Force has also ordered the Seahawk to replace its aging fleet of SH-3s.

Sikorsky has marketed an export version of the Black Hawk, the S-70A. The first few S-70As went to the Republic of the Phillipines Air Force and the Royal Australian Air Force. The majority of all other Australian Black Hawks will be assembled by Hawker de Havilland in Australia. Westland of Great Britain, continuing its long association with Sikorsky, will assemble the helicopter from kits supplied by Sikorsky.

Above: *This SH-60B Seahawk lifts off from its home ship for an exercise run.*

The SH-60B Seahawk fills the Navy's Light Airborne
Multipurpose System (LAMPS) III role.

SIKORSKY UH-60A BLACK HAWK/SH-60B SEAHAWK

Main rotor diameter:	53 ft., 8 in.
Tail rotor diameter:	11 ft.
Length:	50 ft., 0.75 in
Width:	7 ft., 9 in.
Height:	16 ft., 10 in.
Weight (maximum take-off):	16,260 lbs.
Cruising speed:	184 mph
Maximum altitude:	19,000 ft.
Range:	373 miles
Date of first flight:	1974

The engines and exhausts of the UH-60A Black Hawk are positioned and shrouded to reduce its infrared signature.

Above: *With a refueling probe attached, the Black Hawk's range of 373 miles can be greatly extended.*
Left: *The UH-60A Black Hawk was designed to fill the role of the Army's utility tactical transport system.*

Opposite, top: The Black Hawk can place assault, airborne, or special operations forces into whatever position tactics dictate. **Opposite, bottom:** The Black Hawk gives the Army a versatile and powerful workhorse. **Above:** The SH-60B Seahawk expands the Navy's antisubmarine warfare (ASW) capability. Note the AQS-81 Magnetic Anomaly Detector probe behind and beneath the exhaust. **Left:** The SH-60B carries up to 2,000 pounds of electronic equipment in its ASW role.

McDONNELL DOUGLAS AH-64A APACHE

In 1881 in Arizona, the US Sixth Cavalry fought Apaches led by Geronimo, Chato, Nana, and Juh. Exactly 105 years later, the Sixth Cavalry became the first combat-ready unit to field the AH-64A helicopter. The AH-64A was built in Mesa, Arizona, by Hughes Helicopter, Inc., which became McDonnell Douglas Helicopter Company in 1984, and named in honor of the Apache warrior. The AH-64A Apache is the first day/night, all-weather, anti-armor battle helicopter in the U.S. military inventory.

The Apache grew out of the recognition following the Vietnam War that the United States Army needed a helicopter specifically designed for the attack role. After extensive evaluation of several designs, Hughes' YAH-64 prototype was chosen in 1976. The first production Apache was rolled out on September 30, 1983, and the first delivery to the Army was made January 26 of the following year.

To carry out its anti-armor role, the Apache is equipped with the McDonnell Douglas M230 30 millimeter chain gun and up to 16 laser-guided Hellfire antitank missiles, which have a range of more than 3.7 miles and can penetrate the armor of any known main battle tank. The Apache can also provide suppressive fire against concentrations of light armored vehicles and troops. For this task, it uses the chain gun as well as up to 76 2.75-inch folding-fin aerial rockets that can deliver antipersonnel mines or high explosives. Two soldiers can reload or reconfigure the helicopter's weapons systems within ten minutes.

The Apache is also being tested in the air-to-air role and has been approved to fire the Stinger antiaircraft missile. Its M230 30mm chain gun can be used against other helicopters and fixed wing aircraft.

The Apache, while carrying a load of eight Hellfire missiles, 320 rounds of 30mm ammunition, and fuel for 1.83 hours, can climb at the rate of 1,450 feet per minute on what is known as the Army Standard Hot Day, defined as 95 degrees at 4,000 feet altitude. The aircraft can also climb at a

The AH-64A Apache is the first American helicopter built for the antitank warfare role.

Above: *Equipped with extra fuel tanks, the AH-64A can reach any part of a battle zone from the protection of bases deep in the rear.*
Opposite: *The sight of four AH-64A Apaches armed to the teeth would make even the most hardened tank commander blanch.*

rate greater than 3,000 feet per minute in the weather conditions expected to be encountered in central and western Europe—faster than most jet airliners. With external tanks fitted for extended ranges, the Apache is fully capable of flying itself across the Atlantic.

The Apache was designed to be crashworthy. The fixed landing gear can absorb a straight-down impact at 20 feet per second, and the airframe is designed to collapse in on itself, giving the crew a 95 percent probability of walking away from a crash at up to 42 feet per second. The armored crew seats also absorb impact energy. The canopy protects the crew from fatalities in helicopter crashes as well as helping to prevent the cockpit from being crushed in case of a rollover.

The two General Electric T700-701 turboshaft engines provide maximum continuous power of 1,694 horsepower each and drive the rotor system through individual gear boxes and transmissions mounted in the nose. The engines are mounted far apart—6.6 feet—to minimize the chance of enemy fire damaging both engines at

one time. A 125-horsepower auxiliary power unit operates the transmission to start the engines or to provide full electrical power, pressurized air, and hydraulics when the engines are shut down.

The exhaust system is divided into two subsystems. The main exhaust nozzle is immediately followed by three secondary nozzles per engine. In these secondary nozzles, engine cooling air and external air, drawn in through auxiliary inlets, are mixed with the exhaust, reducing exhaust temperature from 1,065 to 580 degrees. This reduces the engine's infrared signature below the level detectable by current heat-seeking guided missiles.

The Apache's main rotor has four blades, each built up from a four-cell box. Stainless steel spars and glass fiber tubes provide reinforcement. The heavy-gauge stainless steel leading edge can withstand striking a tree branch up to two inches in diameter. The trailing edge can withstand damage from .50 caliber machine guns or 23mm high-explosive shells. The tail rotor is composed of two flexible twin-bladed hubs that can be canted from the vertical to reduce noise.

Above: *The AH-64A Apache packs a heavier, more devastating load of firepower than many World War II attack bombers.*

The Apache has two stub wings that provide additional lift. The wings can also serve as attaching points for external fuel tanks or external pylons to carry Hellfire or 2.75-inch rockets. The tail surfaces consist of a fixed vertical stabilizer and a horizontal stabilizer—dubbed a stabilator. The stabilator is mounted aft of the vertical stabilizer and moves as one piece.

Fuel cells are located forward and aft of the ammunition bay. They are self-sealing against .50 caliber rounds and can absorb the impact of rounds up to 23mm. Against 14.5mm armor-piercing rounds, the cells, which are further protected by foam and backing boards, will self-seal to provide a 30-minute fuel supply. Nitrogen gas purging prevents fire in the event of incendiary-round penetration. No provision has been made for air-to-air refueling.

Armor made of boron carbide bonded to Kevlar protects the Apache crew and vital systems. Blast shields, which protect against 23mm or smaller high-explosive incendiary ammunition, separate the pilot and copilot/weapons operator from each

other; thus, both crew members will not be knocked out by a single round. Armored seats and airframe armor can withstand rounds up to .50 caliber of armor-piercing incendiary shot.

The Apache has a wire strike protection system to sever power or other lines during low-level flights or landings. Wire strikes are a major cause of helicopter crashes.

An upgrade program was defined in 1989 and will be implemented to keep the Apache battle worthy in coming years. One new system that will be installed on one-third of all Apaches by 1992 is the Airborne Adverse Weather Weapon System (AAWWS), also called Longbow. Longbow is a highly classified millimeter-wave radar that will enable the Apache crew to detect and kill tanks, missiles, and aircraft, day or night in smoke, fog, or adverse weather.

The AH-64A Apache will be the Army's main battle tank killer well into the 1990s. The helicopter is being distributed throughout the Army, the National Guard, and Army Reserves.

Above: *An Apache takes off for a mission with 16 Hellfire fire-and-forget missiles nestled in its four quadruple launchers.* **Left:** *The Apache's ability to hug the Earth and use every bit of cover is unmatched.*

Above: Clearly seen on this AH-64A is the target acquisition/designation sight and the pilot's night vision sensor mounted on the nose as well as the 30mm chain gun. **Right:** An Apache unleashes a rocket.
Opposite: The pilot and copilot/weapons operator sit in tandem in the Apache. Note the flat plate canopies that reduce glare.

The AH-64A Apache is equipped with an excellent night vision system that magnifies ambient light. A thermal imager allows the weapons operator to identify enemy armor.

McDONNELL DOUGLAS AH-64A APACHE

Main rotor diameter:	48 ft.
Tail rotor diameter:	9 ft., 2 in.
Length:	48 ft., 2 in.
Width:	10 ft., 6 in.
Height:	12 ft., 7 in.
Weight (maximum take-off):	21,000 lbs.
Cruising speed:	184 mph
Maximum altitude:	21,000 ft.
Range:	300 miles
Date of first flight:	1975

Above: The AH-64A Apache is agile enough to literally hop over ridges and other ground features to "ambush" enemy tanks. **Right:** A close-up of the TADS and pilot night vision system.
Opposite: The Army plans to buy more than 1,000 AH-64A Apaches before production ends.

MIL MI-8 HIP/MI-17 HIP-H

The Mil Mi-8, NATO codenamed Hip, is the most numerous transport helicopter in the military services of the Soviet Union, Warsaw Pact nations, and Soviet client states. The Hip is found in service on every inhabited continent except Australia and North America. First produced in 1961, it is still in production in an uprated, more powerful version, the Mi-17, NATO codenamed Hip-H.

The Mi-8 is a transport helicopter with two gas turbine engines that was originally developed from the Mil Mi-4, which was powered by a piston engine. In the West, the Mi-4 was at first mistakenly considered a copy of the Sikorsky H-19 Chickasaw, but the Mi-4 was in fact about three times more powerful. When Mil designers added two gas turbine engines to an improved Mi-4 airframe, they had developed an extremely powerful and versatile helicopter. If a comparison were to be made to a Western helicopter design, the Mil Mi-8 would be broadly similar to the Sikorsky S-61/SH-3 Sea King.

The Mi-8 is powered by two Isotov TV2-117A turboshaft engines developing 1,700 horsepower each. Both engines are mounted above the main cabin/cargo hold area, and the air inlets extend forward to the rear of the cockpit.

The main rotor is five-bladed. The blades are constructed of a single hollow main spar of extruded aluminum alloy and 21 separate pieces of honeycomb construction bolted to the main spar. The main rotor is equipped with standard de-icing equipment. The tail rotor has three blades, which are manufactured in a manner similar to the main rotor's blades. On the Mi-8, the tail rotor is mounted on the right side at the end of the tail boom.

The fuselage is conventional semi-monocoque construction. The tail rotor mounting serves as a vertical stabilizer, and two horizontal stabilizers project from either side of the tail boom just ahead of the tail rotor. The landing gear follows the usual Soviet pattern: The nose wheel is mounted beneath the aft end of the cockpit, and the main landing gear wheels are set on struts projecting from the fuselage. All wheels are nonretractable.

This civilian version of the Mi-8 Hip helicopter is being used to fertilize the fields of a Soviet collective farm.

MIL MI-8 HIP/MI-17 HIP-H

Main rotor diameter:	69 ft., 10.25 in.
Tail rotor diameter:	12 ft., 9.9 in.
Length:	Mi-8: 59 ft., 7.4 in.
	Mi-17: 60 ft., 5.4 in.
Width:	8 ft., 2.5 in.
Height:	18 ft., 6.5 in.
Weight (maximum take-off):	Mi-8: 26,455 lbs.
	Mi-17: 28,660 lbs.
Cruising speed:	140 mph
Maximum altitude:	Mi-8: 14,760 ft.
	Mi-17: 16,400 ft.
Range:	Mi-8: 289 miles
	Mi-17: 307 miles
Date of first flight:	1962

Above: *The Mi-8 Hip-C has been the mainstay of the Soviet assault helicopter fleet since it entered production in 1966. The pods below the wings carry 57mm rockets. The empty clips above usually carry AT-3 Sagger antitank missiles.*

Additional fuel tanks can be mounted on either side of the fuselage. The right auxiliary fuel tank is longer than the left tank to allow the main cabin door to open.

In the cockpit, the pilot and copilot sit side by side and directly behind them is a jump seat for the flight engineer. The cockpit and main cabin can be air-conditioned or heated, but separate equipment must be installed for either function. The main cabin can be configured for cargo or for passengers. In the military version, 24 tip-up seats line each wall. The civilian version can carry 28 passengers in seats mounted four abreast. The civilian helicopter can be differentiated from the military helicopter by the cabin windows. The civilian Hip features large rectangular windows, while the military Hip has round windows with ports that allow troops to fire their weapons during the landing phase of an assault. The military version carries a winch, and the floor has either rings or tie-down bolts for securing cargo. All Mi-8s can be reconfigured for medevac missions and can carry 12 stretchers with provision for medical personnel. The rear clamshell doors in the military

version allow the quick loading of small vehicles and bulky weapons.

The Mi-8 Hip-E is perhaps the most heavily armed helicopter in the world. The Hip-E was designed and built primarily for the assault role. Armament includes a 12.7 millimeter DShK heavy machine gun mounted in the nose beneath the cockpit and aimed from the cockpit. The Hip-E also carries up to 192 57mm free-flight rockets in six rocket launchers. Three launchers are mounted on each side on armament racks projecting from the side of the fuselage. Two AT-2 Swatter guided missiles per rack can also be mounted above the 57mm rocket pods. Other armament observed on the Hip-E includes napalm bombs, general-purpose bombs, and butterfly antipersonnel bombs. After the Afghan resistance fighters were armed with Blowpipe and Stinger one-man antiaircraft missiles, the Hip, as well as all other Soviet aircraft, were quickly fitted with chaff and flare dispensers. The export version of the Mi-8 is configured to carry the AT-3 Sagger antitank guided missile, which is not as sophisticated as the AT-2 Swatter.

The Mi-17 Hip-H is a more powerful version of the Mi-8. It uses two Isotov TV3-117MT turboshaft engines that each produce 1,900 horsepower. The same engines are used in the Mi-14 and the Mi-24. Deflectors protect the engines from sand or other foreign matter during field operations. The Mi-17 has been described as an amalgamation of two aircraft, the airframe of the Mi-8 and the engines of the Mi-24. The Mi-17 has shorter engine air inlets than the Mi-8, and the tail rotor is mounted on the left side of the tail boom. There is little else in appearance to distinguish the Mi-8 from the Mi-17. The extra power provided by the new engines was needed to offset the increased weight of new armor and the addition of a GSh-23 23mm multibarrel gun system. The Mi-17 has also received improvements in avionics and control systems. An auxiliary power unit was added to start the engines in remote areas.

The number of variations of the Mi-8 can be confusing. The Mi-8 Hip-A was the single-engine prototype, and the Hip-B was the twin-engine prototype. The Mi-8 Hip-C became the basic production configuration, best known as an assault transport. The Hip-D is configured for a communications role and can be identified by the additional electronics antennae and rectangular boxes mounted on the external racks. The Mi-8 Hip-E is the current standard assault helicopter in Soviet service; it is the most heavily armed of the Mi-8 series. The Hip-F is similar to the Hip-E but is reserved for export; accordingly, armament and avionics will vary from customer to customer. The Hip-G is an up-rated communications helicopter with doppler radar. The Hip-H is also known as the Mi-17 Hip-H, discussed earlier. The Hip-J and Hip-K are used for communications jamming. The K model can be identified by the large array of usual-shaped Yagi-type antennae mounted on either side of the fuselage.

The Mi-8/Mi-17 series is one of the most successful military helicopters ever. More than 10,000 of the two versions combined have been built. They serve in the armed forces and civil aviation components of at least 39 nations. More than 2,400 Mi-8s and Mi-17s are currently part of 20 helicopter attack regiments that support Soviet ground forces in the field.

MIL MI-24 HIND

The Mi-24, NATO codenamed Hind, has been subject in the past to a number of misinterpretations. It has been characterized as a flying tank, as a gunship, and as an armed troop transport. In fact, it is all of these and more.

The Mi-24 was designed as an armed troop transport to follow on the Mi-8 Hip series. The Soviet Army, after studying American experiences in South Vietnam, recognized a need for a troop transport that could provide its own ground suppression fire. The first version of the Mi-24, the Hind-A, was heavily armed with pods containing 57 millimeter rockets, the AT-2 Swatter anti-tank missile, and 12.7mm machine guns. The main compartment behind the cockpit could hold up to eight fully equipped troops, a full infantry squad, who were trained to fire their weapons through portholes when landing in a hot combat zone. These design parameters made the Mi-24 Hind-A a very large helicopter and therefore more vulnerable to ground fire than Western helicopter designers thought necessary.

The Hind-A carried a crew of three: pilot, co-pilot/weapons operator, and flight engineer. The pilot and copilot/weapons operator sat side by side in a roomy cockpit that was armored for protection against small arms ground fire. The fuselage was conventional semi-monocoque construction. A series of bumps, protrusions, and blisters projecting from the streamlined fuselage provided mountings or shields for a variety of electronic and optical sights, target designators, and communications gear. The Hind's tricycle landing gear was fully retractable.

Two TV2-117A turboshaft engines, the same engines used in the Mi-8 Hip, were mounted atop the main fuselage with an oil cooler bolted on top of the engine. A small auxiliary power unit was set behind the oil cooler and the main rotor.

The main rotor was similar to but smaller than that used in the Mi-8/Mi-17 series. Main rotor blades were made from titanium spars and honeycomb cores covered with glass fiber. A leading edge electric de-icer and anti-erosion strip were included. Balance tabs were found on the trailing edge of all five blades. The tail rotor was mounted on the right side of the swept-back vertical stabilizer, and the tail rotor blades were of aluminum alloy.

Above: More than 2,400 Mi-24 Hind assault helicopters have been built in the Soviet Union since 1976. Below: This Mi-24 Hind was flown to Honduras in December 1988 by a defecting Nicaraguan Sandinista pilot.

MIL MI-24 HIND-D

Main rotor diameter:	55 ft., 9 in.
Tail rotor diameter:	12 ft., 9.5 in.
Length:	57 ft., 5 in.
Width:	6.5 ft. (estimated)
Height:	21 ft., 4 in.
Weight (maximum take-off):	24,250 lbs.
Cruising speed:	183 mph
Maximum altitude:	14,750 ft.
Range:	198 miles
Date of first flight:	1972

Soviet Mi-24 crews from the Cis-Carpathian Military District after a hard day's flying during Operation Karpaty.

Two wings provided nearly one-quarter of the Hind's lift, improving its performance over that of the Mi-8/Mi-17 series. The wings also provided mountings for the variety of weapons the Hind was able to carry and were bent downward to make weapons loading easier.

The Mi-24 Hind-A was deployed to Soviet Army squadrons in East Germany beginning in 1974 to patrol the border between East and West Germany. Experience gained there, and supplemented by actual battle experience in Afghanistan, led to substantial changes in equipment as well as in mission and tactics.

The Hind-D was the result. It is quite similar to the A model except for two major changes. More powerful TV3-117A engines, producing 2,200 horsepower each, were substituted, and the tail rotor was mounted on the left side of the vertical stabilizer to reduce noise. The cockpit was redesigned to meet the needs of its new mission, which is to serve as a flying tank, or gunship. The pilot and copilot/weapons operator no longer sat side by side but rather in tandem with the pilot behind and above the copilot/weapons operator for better all-around visibility. The copilot/weapons operator's station was up-rated with more extensive instrumentation and improved targeting devices. Both crew positions were heavily armored and given their own separate canopies. A four barrel 12.7mm Gatling-type machine gun was mounted in the nose, giving the Hind-D an air-to-air, as well as an air-to-surface, capability. The ability to carry the eight-member infantry squad was retained.

The immediate follow-on to the D model was the Hind-E. The E model was given wingtip launchers and four pylons under the wings that enabled it to carry and launch up to 12 AT-6 Spiral radio-controlled guided missiles. The Hind-F is similar to the Hind-E, but it carries a 30mm twin barrel cannon on the right side of the fuselage. Both versions can carry spare missiles and machine gun ammunition in the main cabin, but the helicopter must land for the crew to reload.

The Mi-24's avionics include VHF and UHF radios, autopilot, radar altimeter, blind-flying instrumentation, automated navigation/map display systems, and in the D and E variations, an effective low-light television camera and receiver system for night operations. The D and E models are also configured with a forward-looking infrared targeting system.

The Hind was king of the hill in Afghanistan until the introduction of one-man antiaircraft missiles like the British Blowpipe and the American Stinger. To counter the infrared-seeking Stinger and Blowpipe, infrared suppressors were mounted on the engine exhausts, and chaff and flare dispensers were made more effective. Tactics were also changed. Rather than a long-glide or low-altitude approach, it was found safer to approach the landing zone at a high altitude and drop in as fast as possible while dispensing flares to decoy the infrared-seeking missiles. These tactics gave up the element of surprise but saved helicopters and crews. By the end of the Soviet combat role in

Afghanistan, more than 200 Mi-24 Hinds had been shot down.

More than 2,400 Mi-24 Hinds in various configurations have been built, and production continues at the rate of about 15 per month. An export version of the Mi-24, a less capable model called the Mi-25, has been sold to other countries within the Soviet sphere of influence. The Mi-25 is distinguished mainly by being configured for the wire-guided AT-3 Sagger antitank missile.

More than 1,100 Hind-D and Hind-E helicopters are in service with the Soviet Army in Europe and southwest and east Asia. Other countries flying the Mi-24 Hind include Warsaw Pact nations Bulgaria, Czechoslovakia, East Germany, Hungary, and Poland. Outside the Warsaw Pact countries, Afghanistan, Algeria, Angola, Cuba, India, Iraq, Mozambique, Nicaragua, North Korea, Vietnam, and South Yemen all fly the Mi-24.

MIL MI-28 HAVOC

As of mid-1989, the Mi-28 Havoc had not yet made its appearance. Western intelligence sources, both classified and open, have been predicting the imminent deployment of the Havoc since the early 1980s. Only a few photographs and illustrations are available. Most sources infer that the Mi-28, NATO codenamed Havoc, is still in prototype testing, but the Defense Department seems to think it could be fielded in late 1989 or 1990.

The great number of helicopters lost to one-man antiaircraft guided missiles in Afghanistan between 1985 and 1988 could possibly be responsible for the delay in introducing the new Mi-28 Havoc. Soviet designers may be seeking new ways to decrease the helicopter's vulnerability to these deadly weapons. Most likely, the new generation of Soviet helicopters will either stand off at some distance or pop up from cover to fire its weapons, rather than orbit the battlefield while delivering assault fire.

Since the Defense Department probably obtained this information of the Mi-28 from actual photographs taken by satellites or reconnaissance aircraft, it seems reasonable to assume that the major details are correct. Other inferences can be drawn from published information.

To start, one of the Mi-24 Hind's greatest drawbacks in combat was its excessive width, which made it a large target for antiaircraft guns and missiles. *Jane's All The World's Aircraft* (1987–88 edition) and the United States Air Force Association's most recent survey of Soviet military aircraft suggest that the Mi-28 will be confined to the ground assault role. If so, it will not need to carry troops, and the wide main cabin can be eliminated. If the tandem cockpit design is retained, which it surely will be, the fuselage would be reduced to almost half the width of the Mi-24 Hind-A.

Most sources seem to think that the Havoc will use the Isotov TV3-117 turboshaft engines, which also power the Mi-24 Hind-C/D/E and the Mi-17 Hip-H. This would be consistent with previous Mil bureau design practice. The two engines would be slung in pods on either side of an extension of the cockpit/main rotor fairing at the top of the fuselage. All pictures released to date show the exhausts angled upward, but not fitted with in-

Above: *This artist's rendering of the new Soviet Mi-28 Havoc, which appeared for the first time in the 1985 edition of* Soviet Military Power, *proved to be remarkably accurate.* **Left:** *The Mi-28 Havoc presents new challenges for NATO.*

Above: *The Mi-28, the new Soviet assault helicopter, carries a single-barrel gun mounted beneath the nose. The window under the nose is probably a day/night vision system.* **Opposite, top:** *The Mi-28 Havoc is expected to be as fully capable in the antitank role as the AH-64A Apache.* **Opposite, bottom:** *This close-up of the Mi-28 shows the heavy armor surrounding the cockpit and the low-mounted main rotor.*

frared suppressors. But combat-ready Mi-28 helicopters would certainly use infrared suppressors. The engine air intakes would likely be fitted with the flattened, cone-shaped dust deflectors developed by the Mil bureau.

The Mi-28 has stubby wings that slant downward, as is the case with the Mi-24, that would provide as much as 25 percent of total lift. The Mi-28 Havoc's wings are swept back, which suggests a higher operating speed than the Mi-24. The Mi-28 will also be fitted with weapons attaching points similar to those used on the Mi-24 Hind-D/E.

The cockpit will probably duplicate the layout found in the Mi-24 except that the pilot and co-pilot/weapons operator positions will be set further back from the nose. The extra room will be used to house electronics and radar. It is likely that the separate armor-protected crew positions will be retained. The canopy will most likely be nonreflective flat glass.

Jane's suggests that a new design for the main and tail rotors will be used but provides no details. The Air Force Association survey states only that

it is new. All available pictures and information indicate that the Mi-28 Havoc has a swept-back vertical stabilizer crossed at the top with a horizontal stabilizer. The three-bladed tail rotor is mounted at the end of the horizontal stabilizer on the right side.

All pictures, from whatever source, show the Mi-28 Havoc armed with a large caliber, single barrel gun mounted in a pod slung beneath the helicopter's nose. The gun will probably be the GSh 23 millimeter or 30mm, which would provide the helicopter with significant air-to-air capability. The Havoc will at least equal, if not surpass, the Mi-24 in weapons-carrying ability. The wings suggest there is room for up to 16 AT-6 Spiral radio/laser-guided antitank missiles, or eight AT-6s and four to eight air-to-air guided missiles, or 64 57mm air-to-ground rockets.

The appearance in military service of the Mi-28 Havoc is only a matter of time. When it is deployed, the Soviets will have gained an edge in ground assault helicopters that the West will have to counter.

MIL MI-28 HAVOC*

Main rotor diameter:	55 ft., 9 in.
Tail rotor diameter:	Not available
Length:	57 ft., 1 in.
Width:	5 ft., 4 in. (less engines)
Height:	15 ft., 3 in.
Weight (maximum take-off):	17,635 lbs.
Cruising speed:	186 mph
Maximum altitude:	Not available
Range:	149 miles
Date of first flight:	1982 or 1983

*All figures are estimates.

KAMOV KA-36 HOKUM

The Kamov Ka-36, NATO codenamed Hokum, is reputed to be the first of a new breed of military helicopters designed primarily for air-to-air combat. As with the Mi-28 Havoc, the imminent deployment of the Ka-36 Hokum has been rumored for years. Only a few photographs and illustrations of the Hokum exist in the open press. While there have been reports of the Havoc flying in Afghanistan, no such reports concerning the Hokum have been made. The fact of the Hokum's existence has been published in *Soviet Military Power,* the annual report by the United States Department of Defense on the state of Soviet military forces, since the 1984 edition. An artist's rendering, believed to be accurate, has been included since the 1987 edition. From the drawings and photographs and the few published reports that contain hard data, it is possible to draw the following conclusions about the Ka-36 Hokum.

The Hokum will be extremely fast for a helicopter, with a speed in excess of 215 miles per hour. This speed is achieved by streamlining the fuselage to a greater degree than past Soviet helicopters and by using quite large wings in proportion to the overall size of the aircraft. These wings could provide as much as 35 to 45 percent of the craft's total lift.

The Hokum has a coaxial counterrotating main rotor. The main rotor system will probably be similar, at least outwardly, to the coaxial counterrotating main rotors used by the Kamov design bureau in the past. The rotor could be particularly close to the one developed for the Ka-27/32 Helix. If so, then the main rotor will consist of two sets of fully articulated three-bladed rotors turning in opposite directions. The blades will be state-of-the-art carbon fiber and honeycomb construction and will probably use the adjustable tab system that the Kamov bureau favors.

Two gas turbine engines will be slung on either side of the fuselage, below the main rotor. It is possible they will be the same TV3-117 series of turboshaft engines that power the Ka-27/32, the Mi-24, and the Mi-28. The Hokum apparently uses a fixed wing aircraft-style tail assembly with conventional vertical and horizontal stabilizers.

This is one of the earliest published photographs of the Soviet Union's new air-superiority helicopter, the Ka-36 Hokum. The counterrotating main rotor system increases speed and eliminates the need for a tail rotor.

The Kamov Ka-36 Hokum is thought to be the first air-superiority helicopter fighter developed, reflecting Soviet concern over NATO developments in antitank helicopters.

The Defense Department pictures show vertical plates at the ends of the horizontal stabilizer.

Judging from the size of the Hokum, it will carry a crew of two: pilot and copilot/weapons operator. The pilot will sit behind and above the copilot/weapons operator. As in the Mi-24 Hind-D/E, the Hokum's cockpit will probably have separate armored compartments for each crew member. The cockpit will most likely be enclosed by an impact-resistant, flat plate canopy. Landing gear will be fully retractable.

The Department of Defense has stated in *Soviet Military Power* and other assessments of the Hokum that no Ka-36 has been observed carrying, or testing, antitank weaponry. Pictures show two guns. One gun, perhaps a 12.7 millimeter

machine gun, protrudes from the left side of the streamlined nose. The other gun is possibly a 23mm or 30mm rapid-firing cannon and is mounted in a weapons pod on the right side of the aircraft below the cockpit. The extra-large wings would certainly provide ample hard point attachments for a range of weaponry from free-flight rockets to such air-to-air missiles as the AA-2 Atoll, the AA-8 Aphid, or the new AA-11 Archer.

As with the Mi-28 Havoc, production and deployment of the Ka-36 Hokum may have been delayed to incorporate lessons learned in Afghanistan. When this new air-to-air combat helicopter is finally introduced into regular service, the Soviets will have a tremendous edge along the forward edge of the battle area. In the West,

the development of an air-combat helicopter has lagged so far behind as to be nonexistent. The only work in this area has been half-hearted testing of the American AH-64A Apache, the UH-60 Blackhawk, the AH-1W SuperCobra, the CH-53 Super Stallion, and the British Lynx 3 for air-to-air combat.

Almost any military helicopter that can handle the payload and associated electronics can be equipped with a rapid-firing cannon, machine guns, and air-to-air missiles. But this does not make a helicopter air-combat worthy any more than hanging weapons on a Cessna 180 would turn it into a fixed wing fighter. Clearly, the Hokum, with its expected speed and agility, will be *the* air-combat helicopter for some time to come.

KAMOV KA-36 HOKUM *

Main rotor diameter:	45 ft., 10 in.
Length:	44 ft., 3.5 in.
Width:	Not available
Height:	17 ft., 8 in.
Weight (maximum take-off):	16,500 lbs.
Cruising speed:	215 mph
Maximum altitude:	Not available
Range:	155 miles
Date of first flight:	Not available

*All figures are estimates.

WESTLAND LYNX

O f the three helicopters that were part of the 1967 Anglo-French helicopter agreement—Puma, Gazelle, and Lynx—the Lynx was the only one to sport a British design. Built as a multirole general-purpose aircraft for the military and civilian marketplace, the Lynx quickly established itself as an agile aircraft capable of a variety of missions.

Over its long history, the Lynx has undergone many updates, upgrades, and modifications. Early models of the Lynx, the British Army AH 1, the British Navy HAS 2, and many export versions, were powered by two Rolls Royce Gem 2 turboshaft engines that develop up to 900 horsepower. Later export versions and most modern aircraft in the British Army or British Navy inventory now feature up-rated Gem 41-1 or 41-2 engines. These newer engines are considerably more powerful and produce either 1,120 horsepower or 1,315 horsepower.

Because the Lynx is a such a versatile helicopter, it performs many roles for both the military and civilian services. In the aircraft's basic configuration, the pilot and copilot are seated side by side, and optional dual controls are available. Normal carrying capacity is up to 10 combat soldiers or, in its medevac role, three stretchers and a medical attendant. The Lynx can haul up to 2,000 pounds of internal cargo or carry up to 3,000 pounds externally via a sling system.

The basic British Army version of the helicopter was called the AH Mark 1. Two up-rated versions have since been produced. The AH Mark 5 had more powerful engines; the AH Mark 7 sported the AH Mark 5's larger engines and also featured an improved tail rotor design with composite blades. The new tail rotor design not only reduced aircraft operating noise but also increased the aircraft's ability to hover for long periods of time while carrying high weight limits. For the anti-armor role, this increased hover time greatly enhanced the helicopter's ability to seek out, wait for, and then destroy enemy tanks.

In the British Navy, the basic Lynx helicopter was called the HAS Mark 2 and was designed for antisubmarine warfare (ASW) duties. But both the British and French Navy versions perform many more missions and duties than simply seeking out and destroying enemy submarines. Lynx variants are capable of search and rescue, reconnaissance, fleet communication, airborne warfare coordination, troop transport, supply replenishment,

Top: *The Westland Sea Lynx, shown here on NATO exercises, is the British Navy's multipurpose helicopter.* **Bottom:** *The Super Lynx was designed to enhance the HAS Mk 2 Sea Lynx's already powerful antisubmarine role. This Super Lynx carries the Sting Ray, a computer-controlled torpedo that seeks out enemy submarines.*

WESTLAND LYNX

Main rotor diameter:	42 ft.
Tail rotor diameter:	7 ft., 3 in.
Length:	Army: 39 ft., 6 in.
	Navy: 39 ft., 1 in.
Width:	Army: 9 ft. 7.75 in.
	Navy: 12 ft., 3.75 in.
Height:	Army: 12 ft.
	Navy: 11 ft., 9.75 in.
Weight (maximum take-off):	Army: 10,000 lbs.
	Navy: 10,500 lbs.
Cruising speed:	Army: 161 mph
	Navy: 144 mph
Maximum altitude:	Army: 10,600 ft.
	Navy: 8,450 ft.
Range:	Army: 392 miles
	Navy: 368 miles
Date of first flight:	1971

fire control, and functioning as missile launch platforms for surface vessel warfare.

Differences between the army and naval versions for the most part can be found on the naval version, which has various ship-borne features that include a beefed-up landing gear and different avionics, cockpit layout, and weapons systems. The aircraft's tail boom and main blades can be folded to make a more compact and easily stowable aircraft, a necessity on ships where space is at a premium.

The versatility of the Lynx allows it to carry a large variety and quantity of weapons systems. Naval versions with antisubmarine or antiship missions will carry one or more types of surface/dipping sonars, reconnaissance pods, sonobuoys, flares and markers, Sting Ray computer controlled torpedoes, Mark 44 homing torpedoes, Mark 11 depth charges, British Aerospace Sea Skua/Aerospatiale AS 15TT/IFV Penguin antiship missiles, 20 millimeter or 30mm cannons, machine gun pods, folding-fin rockets, and Stinger air-to-air missiles for fending off aerial attacks. The Army version of the Lynx offers an equally

wide array of modern weapons systems. Among the armaments it carries are: up to eight TOW missiles with reloads, folding-fin rockets, 20mm or 30mm cannons mounted either in the cabin or on the weapons pylons, two quadruple HOT or RBS-70 missile launchers, General Dynamics Stinger or Mata Mistral antiaircraft missiles, BAe (British Aerospace) Alarm antiradar missiles, machine gun pintle mounts or pod configuration, and a TV reconnaissance camera pod for battlefield surveillance.

Work on the Lynx continues; production is split between Westland, which shoulders 70 percent of the workload, and Aerospatiale, which carries 30 percent of the workload. More than 300 Lynx aircraft are in service worldwide. The new Super Lynx now beginning to appear on the scene features extended range and load capabilities, additional weapons stores, new avionics and detection gear, and an all-weather day/night attack capability. The Super Lynx also has a more efficient tail rotor system and the new Westland-developed swept-tip composite blades for increased performance capabilities.

Above: *The Super Lynx is especially powerful in the antitank role, but it can perform other duties as well, from troop transport to medical evacuation.* **Left:** *This naval version of the Lynx wears French colors and waits aboard ship with blades folded for a call to duty.*

WESTLAND LYNX 3

At first glance, the similarity in appearance of the Westland Lynx 3, a derivative of the Lynx family of helicopters, to other Lynx helicopters is undeniable. The major difference in outward appearance is a twin-finned tail design borrowed from the Westland 30 helicopter design. The new tail provides the helicopter with even more precise handling and agility.

The Lynx 3 comes with two Rolls Royce Gem 60 turboshaft engines that can deliver 1,115 horsepower each. This aircraft, which first flew in 1984, sports a new high-technology composite rotor blade design that is up to 40 percent more efficient than conventional rotor blades. These British Experimental Rotor Program tips are made of a wound filament construction; they hold great promise for a variety of future helicopter designs for increased power and performance.

The helicopter's fuselage features a streamlined pod and boom design constructed from a combination of glass fiber composites and light alloy metal. Able to carry 2,204 pounds of fuel, the helicopter has crash resistant/self-sealing fuel bladders built into its fuselage walls. This feature adds greatly to crew survivability should the helicopter be shot down or forced to make an emergency landing.

Although many of the flight dynamics of the basic Lynx have been retained in the Lynx 3, the overall gross weight of the aircraft has increased by more than 27 percent. This dramatic increase is due to more weapons systems firepower. Westland originally designed the Lynx 3 as an antitank helicopter. But Westland is expanding the flight parameters of the aircraft and offering a naval version that can handle both antisubmarine and antiship roles. Depending on the variant, new and advanced avionics enable the helicopter to go tank or ship hunting in virtually all types of weather, day or night. Numerous night vision and target acquisition systems can be mounted in the nose of the chopper, on the roof above the flight crew, or above the rotor blades.

The armament mainstay for the British Army helicopter is a host of antitank rockets and mis-

The Westland Lynx 3 weighs much more than the basic Lynx, primarily due to the extra firepower of the Lynx 3.

Above: *The Lynx 3 can serve in a variety of roles, from antitank to antisubmarine.* **Opposite:** *TOW, HOT, and Hellfire missiles are just some of the armaments the Lynx 3 can carry.*

siles. The Lynx 3 can carry a full complement of such deadly tank destroyers as the TOW, Hellfire, and HOT missiles. Depending on the helicopter's specific mission, such armaments as folding-fin rockets, cannon pods, machine guns, TV surveillance cameras, chaff dispensers, and air-to-air missiles for self-protection can be added. In the naval version, the latest in computer-controlled torpedoes, homing torpedoes, depth charges, antiship missiles, sonobuoys, dipping sonars, and surface ship radars can be hung on the twin external pylon mounts.

Westland expects the vast array of technological improvements found on the Lynx 3 helicopter to keep the aircraft in production well into the 21st century. The Lynx 3 will be available for export to many nations needing an antiarmor and antisubmarine warfare helicopter of advanced design.

WESTLAND LYNX 3

Main rotor diameter:	42 ft.
Tail rotor diameter:	8 ft.
Length:	39 ft., 6.8 in.
Width:	10 ft.
Height:	10 ft., 10 in.
Weight (maximum take-off):	13,000 lbs.
Cruising speed:	172 mph
Maximum altitude:	10,600 ft.
Range:	385 miles
Date of first flight:	1984

AEROSPATIALE SA 316B ALOUETTE III

The Alouette series of helicopters from the French company Aerospatiale has roots stretching back to the 1950s. This line of helicopters contributed significantly to the postwar reconstruction of the French aircraft industry. First came the simple, yet proven design of the SE-3120 Alouette Lark. Then came the improved Alouette II Astazou, which boasted a more economical engine and a new centrifugal clutch. Aerospatiale then jumped forward to the Alouette III. Many called it the big sister to the smaller Alouette II, and the resemblance was unmistakable. Although the tail boom had been enclosed and the cabin area expanded to seat seven people, the Alouette III's superb capabilities were definitely and undeniably Aerospatiale. The helicopter became an overnight success.

The Alouette III helicopter first flew in February 1959 and soon proved its flight capabilities through a variety of publicity stunts such as landing and taking off with full maximum loads from atop Mont Blanc in the French Alps. That kind of power spurred sales to a variety of civilian and military marketplaces that operate in hot and/or high-altitude environments, such as Switzerland, Saudi Arabia, India, and Zaire. By the time French production came to an end in May 1985, a total of 1,455 Alouette IIIs had been delivered to civilian and military forces in 74 different countries.

The Alouette III's power, and therefore its success, was derived from a light turbine helicopter powerplant developed by the Turbomeca company—the first engine manufacturer to develop such an engine. This engine, which was used throughout the 316B series of aircraft, developed 870 horsepower and enabled the helicopter to cruise along at a steady 115 miles per hour for ranges in excess of 300 miles.

Even after the French shut down their production lines, numerous other nations continued to produce the Alouette III under license from Aerospatiale. Switzerland built a total of 60 aircraft, and Romania built nearly 200 aircraft in both a civilian and military version. The Romanian military model is called the IAR-317 Airfox. The only group now still producing the Alouette III design is

AEROSPATIALE SA 316B
ALOUETTE III

Main rotor diameter:	36 ft., 1.75 in.
Tail rotor diameter:	6 ft., 3.25 in.
Length:	32 ft., 11 in.
Width:	8 ft., 6.25 in.
Height:	9 ft., 10 in.
Weight (maximum take-off):	3,630 lbs.
Cruising speed:	115 mph
Maximum altitude:	10,500 ft.
Range:	307 miles
Date of first flight:	1959

This ski-equipped Alouette III, belonging to the French police, patrols in the French Alps.

Above: *Licensed versions of the Alouette III are built in India, Switzerland, and Romania.*

the HAL company of India, which has produced more than 300 helicopters under the Indian designation Chetak.

Since Aerospatiale has ceased production of the aircraft, further improvements to the Alouette III will be limited to modifications by owners. India and Romania have plans for revised avionics, which are basic compared with other helicopters in use today. Only a few Alouettes have much in the way of sophisticated electronics and avionics beyond a basic radio, rudimentary radars, and targeting/sensor systems.

The Alouette III had broad demonstrated capabilities, and it was quickly outfitted with a variety of armaments and weapon systems. In fact, the Alouette II and Alouette III were the first helicopters to be deployed into service carrying guided missiles. Known as the SS-10, this wire-guided antitank missile was carried by the aircraft for several years. Later, the Alouette II and Alouette III were armed with the larger and heavier AS-11. The AS-11 remains the standard armament today, and the Alouette III can carry up to four missiles—two on each side of the aircraft. The

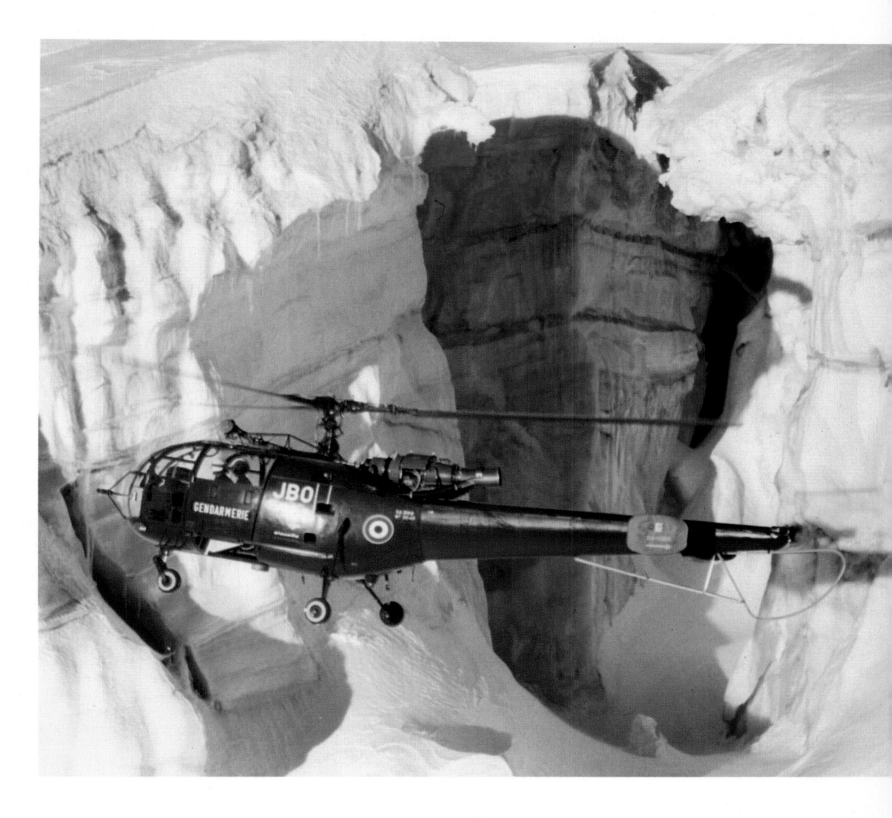

weapons operator, who sits beside the pilot, controls firing with the APX-Bezu 260 gyrostabilized sight mounted on the cockpit roof.

Gun weaponry for the Alouette III began with pintle- or tripod-mounted machine guns capable of firing from the side door of the aircraft. A standard item in the weaponry department included the 7.62 millimeter AA-52 gun that had a capacity of 1,000 rounds; it was fired either through the opened or removed door or through a gun portal aperture cut into the door. For heavier firepower, the Alouette III could also be outfitted with a variety of 20mm cannons that had a magazine capacity of up to 480 rounds. Additional weapons systems that can be hung on the outside of the helicopter include a variety of rocket launchers, HOT missiles, Matra Mistral guided missiles, AT-3 Sagger antitank missiles, gun pods, and up to two antisubmarine Mark 44 torpedoes.

Overall, there were few missions in the Alouette III's day that the aircraft couldn't handle. Antitank, antisubmarine, search and rescue, light attack, or medevac were all part of its job. The Alouette III continues to fulfill those roles.

Above: *The military version of the Alouette III can be equipped with a variety of weapon systems, including TOW or HOT antitank missiles.*

AEROSPATIALE SA 341/342 GAZELLE

Development of the agile Aerospatiale Gazelle started in the mid-1960s. The French Army issued a requirement for a light observation helicopter that was faster and even more agile than the helicopters being produced in the Alouette series. There were major differences between the new design, which was designated the X-300, and older helicopter model introductions. A new streamlined fuselage replaced the bubble-type cabin/cockpit area. The open metal latticework tail boom was enclosed and streamlined. A rigid rotor design with glass fiber composite blades, which the German company Messerschmitt-Bolkow-Blohm had pioneered, and an encased—or shrouded—tail rotor blade design called fenestron (fan-in-fin) were added.

Under a 1967 Anglo-French agreement, the Gazelle was co-produced by Aerospatiale and Westland Helicopters. The Gazelle became a mainstay of helicopter technology for both French and British forces. Known as the SA 341, the helicopter soon became a standard for all British services. In the British Army Air Corps, the aircraft was used as an observation ship. In the Royal Air Force and the Navy Fleet Air Arm, the Gazelle was used for helicopter training. The RAF took the attributes of the Gazelle further and used the helicopter as a communications platform and for forward air controller missions.

These early SA 341 Gazelles came equipped with a single Turbomeca Astazou turboshaft engine that delivered 590 horsepower, which provided excellent power, performance, and agility for its time. Versions developed and introduced later were improved in their power and are known as the SA 342 model. The SA 342 comes with an engine that develops up to 858 horsepower. Other changes in the newer model include a redesigned fenestron tail rotor, a higher gross take-off weight, and an option for an extended cabin.

The Gazelle's design is conventional. It features an airframe made from light alloy metals and a glazed cockpit cabin area with transparent moldings held in place by a welded frame. The floor area and center fuselage are made of a honeycomb construction, and the tail boom is a sheet alloy metal design. Blades can be folded if re-

The Aerospatiale Gazelle is a multirole helicopter that serves well in the antitank role. This Gazelle is equipped with HOT anti-armor missiles in twin launchers.

Above: *The Gazelle was originally intended to replace the Alouette as the light observation helicopter in the French Army.*

quired. Unless ordered otherwise, all Gazelles feature standard skids on which small landing wheels can be added to provide additional taxiing capability. For on-the-water operations and special missions, the helicopter can be fitted with pontoon floats and underwater beacon markers for special forces frogmen.

The basic configuration of the Gazelle consists of a pilot and copilot in side-by-side seating, each with separate systems to fly the aircraft. In the rear, a three-passenger bench can be folded down or removed to accommodate cargo-carrying requirements. In addition to its internal cargo load, the Gazelle can carry up to 1,500 pounds of additional cargo slung externally from a center fuselage hook. When pressed into search and rescue operations, a hoist able to lift 350 pounds can be installed for lifting downed personnel. When the aircraft is configured for medevac missions, the pilot seat on the left can be removed, creating enough room for two stretchers and a medical attendant.

Gazelles have remained up-to-date in terms of avionics. All are equipped with night-operation packages that include standard radios and additional instrumentation that enables the pilot to fly in virtually all weather conditions. The latest radios, sensors, radars, targeting systems, and communications/enemy detection packages can be retrofitted into the Gazelle for a variety of special mission requirements and options.

When properly outfitted, the Gazelle can perform a variety of attack and fighting missions. In its antitank role (known as ALAT, or Army Light Aviation), the helicopter is called the SA 342M and is equipped with a gyrostabilized sighting system. The system is installed in the roof of the cockpit and is designed with optics that either the pilot or copilot can use when functioning as the gunner. Standard antitank weaponry includes two twin HOT missile launchers, two TOW-2 missile launcher platforms, and the Soviet-made AT-3 Sagger antitank missile. Other standard armament for the helicopter, as determined by its mission, includes a variety of tubular/rail munitions, numerous 20 millimeter cannons, wire-guided missiles, and four different versions of air-to-ground unguided rockets. For self-protection, the Gazelle carries two types of air-defense missiles, the British Blowpipe and the French Matra Mistral. The aircraft is armed with a variety of gun systems, including standard 7.62mm/.50 caliber machine gun options and a 7.62mm minigun that is part of a new turret system that can be jettisoned. The Gazelle can also carry various tactical reconnaissance camera pods.

Nearly 1,200 Gazelles have been produced for 36 nations. The helicopter remains in production and is likely to continue to be upgraded well into the next century with new weapons systems, sensors, electronic warfare packages, and radars.

Above: *ALAT (French Army Light Aviation) uses the Gazelle in roles ranging from anti-armor to close support of ground troops.* **Left:** *The HOT anti-armor missile installed in its storage and launch tubes attached to the twin launchers mounted on either side of the Gazelle.*

The Gazelle is fast and agile enough to be a real threat to Warsaw Pact armored forces.

AEROSPATIALE SA 341/ 342 GAZELLE

Main rotor diameter:	34 ft., 5.5 in.
Tail rotor diameter:	2 ft., 3.3 in.
Length:	31 ft., .2 in.
Width:	6 ft., 8.5 in.
Height:	10 ft., 5.5 in.
Weight (maximum take-off):	4,410 lbs.
Cruising speed:	161 mph
Maximum altitude:	13,450 ft.
Range:	440 miles
Date of first flight:	1967

This page: *Advances in digital electronics have eased the pilot's burden by grouping controls and providing video screens that display only that information the pilot needs at the moment.* **Opposite, top:** *The Gazelle's ability to hide in ground cover makes it a dire threat to enemy armored vehicles.* **Opposite, bottom:** *Among the nations flying the Gazelle are France, Great Britain, Yugoslavia, and Egypt.*

AEROSPATIALE SA 365 DAUPHIN/PANTHER

To keep track of all the helicopter variants within the Aerospatiale Dauphin series practically requires a scorecard; there are a host of models and changes within the basic group. The basic aircraft is the SA 365N Dauphin 2, and it is designed as a multirole transport. It remains in full production today.

The helicopter features the distinctive fenestron tail rotor with 11 high-speed blades that are articulated for pitch change. The aircraft also sports a large vertical tail fin and twin horizontal stabilizers as part of the shrouded tail rotor. Power in the basic SA 365 version is derived from two Turbomeca 912 horsepower turboshaft engines, but in the United States Coast Guard version known as the SA 366, power comes from two Avco Lycoming 680 horsepower engines. The four main rotor blades are of a composite design and feature some of the latest technology, including a NOMEX honeycomb filling. The blades attach to a Starflex glass-and-carbon fiber rotor hub that has a quick disconnect pin system for easy replacement and virtually no maintenance.

With the Dauphin's clean aerodynamic fuselage and retractable tricycle landing gear, the helicopter offers excellent performance and handling. The helicopter has a standard flight crew of two and, depending on how the aircraft is configured, can carry up to 14 passengers.

For military service, the Dauphin can be used for transport, attack, medevac, and search and rescue. In service with Saudi Arabia, the Dauphin is used in the antiship role and is called the SA 365F/AS.15TT model. Similar in its basic configuration to other Dauphin models, this version is equipped to carry up to 4 AS.15 antiship missiles on lateral pylons. Also in service with the United States Coast Guard, the helicopter is designated the HH-65A Dolphin 2. The Coast Guard has ordered and received 99 of the aircraft for use in short-range recovery duties. The HH-65A can perform search and rescue operations from shore or ship, or drug interdiction missions in conjunction with law enforcement organizations.

The Aerospatiale SA 365 Panther, an upgraded version of the earlier Dauphin, first flew in 1986.

The Dauphin 2 is a formidable weapons platform. Depending upon the mission, the Dauphin can be outfitted with a variety of weaponry, including antiship missiles, ship and submarine torpedoes, stabilized day/night gun sights, a 20 millimeter cannon, a 7.62mm machine gun, three types of 68mm rocket pods, quadruple TOW missile launchers, and quadruple HOT missile launchers. The aircraft can also carry submarine sonobuoys, surveillance radars, and camera pods.

Aerospatiale has used the basic design of the Dauphin to introduce a new variant that is built for fighting and surviving in a combat environment. Called the Panther, its basic configuration is nearly identical to the Dauphin, but technical designs have placed a much greater emphasis on battlefield survivability. A production model first flew in 1986, and the Panther went into production in 1988.

To increase strength and reduce weight, the Panther makes much greater use of composite materials than the existing Dauphin helicopters. These composites and special radar-absorbing coatings on the helicopter's exterior greatly reduce the aircraft's radar signature, making the Panther difficult to detect. Inside, both crew seats are armored and are designed to withstand crashes or impacts up to 15 G's. Key components around the engines and throughout the many flight control systems are also protected with a variety of armor.

The Panther will serve in a variety of missions that could include assault transport, ground attack, search and rescue, electronic warfare, aerial combat post, medevac, cargo transport, target designation, and armed reconnaissance. Of course, the Panther can carry the entire assortment of weaponry available on the basic Dauphin helicopter as well as additional sensors and electronics.

At present, nearly 400 Dauphins have been built or ordered. This number also includes aircraft that are in production in China, where the helicopter is called the Harbin Z-9. A total of 37 different nations use Dauphin variants in many civilian and military applications. Competition in the multipurpose helicopter arena is fierce, but the Dauphin and Panther have established solid reputations for performance and versatility. Production is expected to continue well into the late 1990s and beyond.

The Panther's crew, engines, and vital electronics are protected by armored seats and panels.

AEROSPATIALE SA 365 DAUPHIN/PANTHER

Main rotor diameter:	39 ft., 2 in.
Tail rotor diameter:	3 ft., 7.5 in.
Length:	38 ft., 2 in.
Width:	10 ft., 6.5 in.
Height:	11 ft., 6.5 in.
Weight (maximum take-off):	9,039 lbs.
Cruising speed:	176 mph
Maximum altitude:	11,810 ft.
Range:	530 miles
Date of first flight:	1972

Above: *The Dauphin was designed and built to be a more capable replacement for the Alouette III.* **Right:** *This Dauphin is being used as a flying test bed to develop a new fly-by-wire control system for future helicopters.*

Above: *In the naval role, the Dauphin has been equipped for both antisubmarine and antiship warfare. This Dauphin fires an Aerospatiale AS.15TT antiship missile.*
Left: *The Aerospatiale company is intent on improving the performance and speed of the Dauphin design. This helicopter, fitted with a five-bladed rotor, is the DTP X 380.*

AEROSPATIALE AS 350/355 ECUREUIL

The AS 350/355 Ecureuil, or Squirrel, was originally designed as a successor to the Aerospatiale Alouette series. The AS 350/355 Ecureuil is similar in size to the SA 341/342 Gazelle but features a completely new design sporting technological improvements that are designed to decrease operating costs, maintenance requirements, and noise.

The AS 350, a light utility multirole helicopter, flew for the first time in June 1974 with one 641 horsepower Turbomeca turboshaft engine. The AS 355 is a twin-engine version of the same aircraft that is marketed in the United States as the Twinstar helicopter and elsewhere throughout the world as the Ecureuil 2. Power for the AS 355 comes from two Allison 250-C20F turboshaft engines that develop 420 horsepower each. The engines give the Ecureuil the power to climb at a rate of nearly 1,300 feet per minute. Recently, Aerospatiale upgraded the powerplant package and is now producing the Ecureuil series with new 509 horsepower Turbomeca TM 319 engines.

Both the 350 and 355 versions feature a rotor hub made of a glass-and-carbon fiber composite design called Starflex. The simple gearbox features only nine gearwheels, and the simple transmission has nine bearings. These previous features, coupled with three advanced design rotor blades that are manufactured by a computer-controlled production process, make the aircraft economical to operate and easy to maintain. The fuselage is covered with a thermoformed plastic instead of light alloy honeycomb panels. The aircraft is configured for a crew of two.

For civilian use, the aircraft is ideal for oil platform transportation, executive transport, news reporting, and law enforcement patrols. The Ecureuil can accommodate four passengers. For cargo transport, the helicopter can be ordered with a large sliding door on each side, removable seats, and an exterior cargo hoist hook. For rescue operations, an electric rescue hoist is also available. A water drop fire fighting system and an agricultural spray tank system are also offered.

In the military arena, both the AS 350 and AS 355 feature advanced electronics that can be tailored to order. In addition to standard flight equipment packages, the Ecureuil can be equipped

The Aerospatiale AS 350 Ecureuil (Squirrel) is a light multirole helicopter. This antitank version is equipped with TOW missiles in twin launchers.

Above: *The Aerospatiale AS 355 Ecureuil is sold in the United States as the Twinstar and elsewhere as the Ecureuil 2.* **Opposite:** *This Ecureuil 350 L1 uses a rotor hub of carbon-glass composites in a design called the Starflex.*

with full infrared instrumentation, radar altimeter, night-vision goggles, and electronic targeting sensors. The aircraft can be used for armed reconnaissance, light attack, target designation, search and rescue, and cargo transport.

Virtually all military versions of the helicopter are equipped with pylon adapters and attachments that allow weaponry to be pointed only straight ahead. This small lightweight helicopter can be armed to the teeth for a variety of light attack missions. In the anti-armor role, the aircraft can carry twin HOT or TOW wire-guided missile launchers on each side. For soft targets, rocket launchers, machine guns, and cannon pods are attached. Helicopters will have to be able to fight and survive aerial combat, and the Ecureuil can

be outfitted with such air-to-air defensive missiles as the Matra Mistral and General Dynamics Stinger.

The AS 350/355, a high-speed and excellent flier, is a popular choice for more than 30 nations; some 2,000 AS 350/355 helicopters have been ordered for both civilian and military use. The Ecureuil is an ideal choice for a variety of light and tactical military applications. With the twin TM-319 engines now available on the AS 355, orders are expected to remain steady for many years to come. Production lines will continue to operate both in France and under license in Brazil. In Brazil, the AS 350, built by Helibras, is called the CH-50 Esquilo, and two versions of the twin engine AS 355 are designated the CH-55 or VH-55 Esquilo.

AEROSPATIALE AS 350/355 ECUREUIL

Main rotor diameter:	35 ft., .75 in.
Tail rotor diameter:	6 ft., 1.25 in.
Length:	35 ft., 10.5 in.
Width:	5 ft., 10.75 in.
Height:	10 ft., 11.5 in.
Weight (maximum take-off):	AS 350: 4,850 lbs.
	AS 355: 5,732 lbs.
Cruising speed:	AS 350: 144 mph
	AS 355: 139 mph
Maximum altitude:	15,000 ft.
Range:	AS 350: 407 miles
	AS 355: 437 miles
Date of first flight:	1974

When equipped with a day/night sighting system (cylindrical object above the cockpit) and twin launchers for TOW missiles, the "Squirrel" becomes a tiger.

Above: *Aerospatiale developed the Orchidee battlefield surveillance system; it will be mounted on the Ecureuil and also used by the French Army.* **Right:** *The Turbomeca Arriel 1D turboshaft engine powers the Ecureuil antitank gunship.*

Above: *The Aerospatiale Ecureuil 2 civilian version is used in roles from offshore resupply to air ambulance.* **Left:** *The Aerospatiale AS 350 Ecureuil lacks a fairing over the engine exhaust and has a single engine, distinguishing it from the Ecureuil 2 version.*

AEROSPATIALE AS 332 SUPER PUMA

The Puma, Super Puma, and Super Puma Mark II series of helicopters from Aerospatiale result from taking a good design and making continual modifications and refinements. The improvements have kept the aircraft current for a variety of missions. Today's AS 332 Super Puma, its origins dating back to the mid-1960s, may superficially look like the earlier SA 330 Puma, but there are many significant improvements and differences.

Although the older Puma was a fine helicopter in many respects, Aerospatiale decided in 1974 that an improved aircraft would be more competitive in the military and civilian marketplaces. The Super Puma, first flown in September 1978, was the result; production models were flying by February 1980. The Puma was originally designed as an all-weather tactical medium-lift helicopter for the French Army ALAT (Army Light Aviation). Many small changes that improved crash safety, reduced operational noise, decreased maintenance requirements, and increased payload capacity helped turn the Puma into the Super Puma. Important power increases in the engines offered significant performance improvements over the original Puma. The Super Puma carries two internally mounted Turbomeca Makila IA1 engines, raising power to 1,877 horsepower from 1,780 horsepower.

Five modern versions of the Super Puma are available today. The AS 332B is the basic military version. It is capable of carrying up to 21 combat troops with its crew of two. The AS 332F is the naval version and features a deck-landing assistance device for ship-borne operations, special anticorrosion metal treatments, and a folding tail rotor pylon for compact storage. The naval version is built for everything from antiship and antisubmarine warfare to search and rescue. The AS 332L is a civilian version of the Super Puma. The cabin, which can accommodate up to 24 passengers, has been stretched 2.5 feet and features two additional windows as well as increased fuel capacity. The AS 332M features the extended cabin of the AS 332L but is built as a military transport aircraft that can haul up to 25 combat soldiers.

The Aerospatiale 332 Super Puma made its first flight in 1978.

Above: *This Super Puma is equipped with ice/debris inlet filters that provide increased capability in winter or Arctic conditions and low-level flying.* **Right:** *The Super Puma was intended to be an all-weather, medium-lift tactical helicopter for the French Army; it succeeded beyond all expectations.*

The fifth version is the new Super Puma Mark II. The Mark II features an improved new main rotor system that will enhance performance and economy without changing or modifying the aircraft's basic powerplants. Several significant modifications have resulted in a new and lighter design that complements the increase of 1.6 feet in fuselage length. The longer fuselage is necessary to accommodate the slightly longer rotor blades. In addition to increased performance, the Mark II will offer increased range, an autopilot feature with new cockpit displays, and additional avionics. The Super Puma Mark II is expected to begin production in 1990.

A future change may include the battlefield surveillance system Orchidee (Obersavtoire Radar Coherent Heliporte d'Investigation Des Elements Ennemis). This system will be used to coordinate French ground forces. Orchidee uses a highly advanced doppler radar system to locate enemy troop concentrations, convoys, or movements as far as 60 miles behind enemy lines while the helicopter itself is more than 25 miles inside its own lines and operating at an altitude of almost 10,000 feet. The surveillance radar device is mounted under the rear of the helicopter's cabin area and swings down into place via a rotating mount. This system has been in operational field testing since 1986 and could begin appearing by the mid-1990s on new helicopters ordered by the French Army. It is anticipated the French will replace their

aging fleet of SA 330 Puma helicopters with Orchidee-equipped Super Pumas.

While most Super Pumas are unarmed, they are heavily laden with a host of avionics and defensive devices. Featuring the latest in communications gear, radars, sensors, and even sonars, the Super Puma can fill a variety of military missions. If an armed version is desired, the Super Puma can be equipped to carry such modern weaponry as a 20 millimeter cannon, machine guns, rocket launchers, Mistral missiles, reconnaissance camera pods, doppler radar systems for battlefield surveillance, two Sea Skua or Exocet antiship missiles, and up to two parachute-equipped acoustic antiship torpedoes. When used for antisubmarine warfare operations, the Super Puma can carry sonobuoys, dipped sonar detectors, and the latest in antisubmarine torpedo weaponry.

More than 350 AS 332 Super Pumas have been delivered to or are on order by nearly 40 military forces from around the world. Production is taking place under license in Indonesia, and assembly is taking place under license in Spain. The Super Puma series of helicopters will continue to be one of the most widely used medium-lift models for many years to come. Aerospatiale officials believe there are future modifications and variants that will keep the aircraft current well into the early part of the 21st century.

AEROSPATIALE AS 332
SUPER PUMA

Main rotor diameter:	51 ft., 2.25 in.
Tail rotor diameter:	10 ft.
Length:	50 ft., 11.5 in.
Width:	12 ft., 5.25 in.
Height:	16 ft., 1.75 in.
Weight (maximum take-off):	19,841 lbs.
Cruising speed:	156 mph
Maximum altitude:	11,480 ft.
Range:	384 miles
Date of first flight:	1978

The Super Puma forms the transportation mainstay of the French Army's Rapid Action Force (FAR).

MESSERSCHMITT-BOLKOW-BLOHM BO 105

The concept of the Messerschmitt-Bolkow-Blohm (MBB) Bo 105 helicopter was launched in 1962. It was one of the first major post-war aircraft design and development programs by the Federal Republic of Germany (West Germany). The government contract called for an advanced rotor design that would feature a rigid hub and composite blades. The idea behind the rigid, or hingeless, hub concept was to keep the blades from flapping and dragging. The blades were to be cantilevered from the hub itself and would be capable of changes in pitch only. The advantages of such a system ranged from increased aircraft stability to greater maneuverability. The reduction in rotor blade/hub moving parts would also improve maintenance.

While research into the rigid hub design continued, various Bo 105 prototypes were flown that used existing technology. In February 1967, the first helicopter using advanced design features flew. Its technology included a rigid titanium hub with feathering hinges only and flexible glass fiber blades. Since 1970, all Bo 105s have featured NACA 23012 "droop snoot" rotor blades.

Except for the hub and rotor blade, the helicopter is conventional in design. The fuselage and tail boom are of a light alloy. The fuselage features a titanium deck under the helicopter's engines and glass-fiber-reinforced cowling panels. The landing gear consists of simple skids to which emergency quick-inflation flotation bags can be attached for on-the-water operations.

In the standard configuration, the pilot and co-pilot sit side by side. Virtually the entire fuselage behind the seats is available for cargo and baggage, and the aircraft has large clamshell doors in the rear and two large sliding doors on the side for easy access to the cargo area. The rear bench seat can be removed to carry cargo or stretchers. In armed versions, the rear cargo area is usually filled with mission equipment. All versions have excellent external lighting systems for night land-

The MBB Bo 105 serves in the West German Army as the PAH-1. In the Bo 105's anti-armor configuration, it carries six HOT missile tubes.

The MBB Bo 105 was designed as a multiple-role helicopter, performing antitank, liaison, surveillance, search and rescue, and gunship missions.

ings and operations. Various optional equipment packages for tailoring the aircraft to a variety of missions include external loudspeaker, rescue hoist, cargo loading hook, auxiliary fuel tanks in the cargo compartment, fuel jettison system, and folding main rotor.

The Bo 105 features two Allison 250-C20B turbine engines delivering 420 horsepower each, which gives the aircraft a very high rate of climb and excellent maneuverability. The Bo 105 can climb at 600 feet per minute at takeoff and maintain a steady rate of climb at maximum power of a very quick 1,575 feet per minute.

The aircraft is able to accept a variety of armament. Main armament for the antitank attack version includes up to six HOT missiles or eight TOW missiles. For missions involving "soft targets," such as troop concentrations, armored personnel carriers, military convoys, and covert/special forces operations, most weapons stores can be hung on external hangers. Options include nearly the entire spectrum of air-to-ground rockets, 20 millimeter cannons, various machine guns and machine gun pods, Stingers, and chaff and flare dispensers.

In the communications and avionics department, the Bo 105 can be fitted with virtually all state-of-the-art equipment. Complete day-and-night, all-weather avionics enable the pilot to operate the aircraft under almost any adverse conditions of darkness and weather. For combat, the aircraft is equipped with a variety of sensors, optics, and self-protection devices, which can include thermal imaging equipment, night goggles for the pilot and copilot, laser range finders, stabilized gun sights, and electronic countermeasure systems.

Designed as a multirole light helicopter, the Bo 105's various missions have included antitank, observation, armed reconnaissance, search and rescue, and law enforcement. The Bo 105 continues in production today, and more than 1,200 have been built and delivered to 37 different nations. For the future, MBB plans to offer upgrades to the existing fleet of helicopters. Upgrades will include engines with more power, new rotor blades for increased performance, and other changes that will increase the aircraft's take-off weight. The additional payload capacity could be used to carry more fuel, additional armaments, or high-load weights. Upgrades will begin in 1990, and all indications are that this small and agile helicopter will continue in military and civilian service for many years to come.

Above: The Colombian Navy uses several MBB Bo 105 helicopters to watch for illicit drug smuggling activity. **Left:** The MBB Bo 105 can carry a wide range of armaments: HOT missiles, TOW missiles, Stingers, 2.75-inch rockets, and a variety of chain guns and cannons.

The MBB Bo 105 is a potent addition to NATO's anti-armor weapons arsenal.

MESSERSCHMITT-BOLKOW-BLOHM BO 105

Main rotor diameter:	32 ft., 3.5 in.
Tail rotor diameter:	6 ft., 2.75 in.
Length:	28 ft., 1 in.
Width:	8 ft., 3.5 in.
Height:	9 ft., 10 in.
Weight (maximum take-off):	5,291 lbs.
Cruising speed:	150 mph
Maximum altitude:	17,000 ft.
Range:	357 miles
Date of first flight:	1967

MESSERSCHMITT-BOLKOW-BLOHM/KAWASAKI BK 117

The Messerschmitt-Bolkow-Blohm/Kawasaki BK 117 combines German and Japanese aeronautic talents and abilities. In 1974, Kawasaki of Japan was working on a seven- to nine-passenger helicopter designated the KH-7; at the same time, the West German firm of Messerschmitt-Bolkow-Blohm (MBB) was working on a similar design called the BK 107. Realizing they would be competing head-to-head, the two companies agreed in 1977 to jointly produce a helicopter called the BK 117. It was agreed MBB would produce the main and tail rotors, control systems, tail boom, landing skids, engine compartment firewalls and cowlings, and hydraulics as well as oversee the integration of all these systems. Kawasaki would make the fuselage, transmission, electrical and fuel systems, and all other standard items required for flight.

Only a limited number of the helicopters have been manufactured to date, and the actual process of building the aircraft is the single-source method. Each company produces the components it has developed, and those parts are then exchanged for production parts made by the partner. Two final assembly lines are currently in use: MBB uses its plant in Donauworth and Kawasaki uses its Gifu factory.

The BK 117 can seat seven, and in many respects, the BK 117 is an enlarged Bo 105 helicopter. It uses the Kawasaki transmission system, but the main rotor group is almost identical to the latest Bo 105 offering. The aircraft features larger blades that are fitted with anti-vibration weights. The anti-erosion strips on the blades are of stainless steel.

The BK 117 features a nose section that is long, wide, and very streamlined. The tail boom is thin and streamlined and features a horizontal

The BK 117 was designed as a larger, more capable follow-on to the MBB Bo 105. Note the .50 caliber machine gun turret beneath the nose.

Above: *The BK 117 can carry nearly 700 pounds more of payload than the Bo 105.* **Opposite, top:** *The BK 117 carries the Multipurpose Delivery System (the brackets on either side of the helicopter), which can carry 2.75-inch rockets, 68mm rockets, or TOW or HOT missiles.* **Opposite, bottom:** *This M159-C1 launcher carries 19 2.75-inch rockets for use against unarmored targets.*

stabilizer with delta-shaped fins that are sharply inclined for greater stability. Except for the horizontal stabilizer, which is made from composites, the aircraft's airframe and primary structure are made of conventional metal alloys. Several areas of the helicopter's skin are reinforced with Kevlar for strength.

Two Avco Lycoming LTS 101-650B-1 turboshaft engines that deliver 550 horsepower each power this multipurpose helicopter. The aircraft can climb at nearly 2,350 feet per minute. The BK 117 has two independent fuel-feeding systems and a common main fuel tank that holds 160 gallons.

Avionics and state-of-the-art communications equipment are available, as well as all such modern navigation aids as laser/doppler system, radar altimeter, transponder, Navstar, Loran, and AHRS (Attitude/Heading Reference System). The military version, called the BK 117A-3M, will have weapons control avionics, a host of targeting computers, electronic warfare equipment and jammers, and either a roof-mounted stabilized sight or mast-mounted sight system.

The BK 117 can carry a variety of armament options, including either HOT or TOW missiles in a quad launcher configuration. The aircraft can be fitted with 2.75-inch folding-fin rockets, 68 millimeter rockets, CASA 80mm rockets, two Stinger air-to-air missile launchers, and the SURA 81mm rocket system. Gun systems range from standard Rheinmetall or Oerlikon 20mm cannons to General Electric 7.62mm miniguns.

In the military configuration, the BK 117 would sport dual pilot controls. If stripped of all military weapons systems, the helicopter could carry up to 11 combat soldiers.

Overall, the BK 117 shows much promise as either an armed or unarmed multipurpose helicopter. The aircraft can function in a variety of roles, including fire fighting, law enforcement, cargo transport, and search and rescue. However, interest has been somewhat limited; fewer than 50 commercial models and no military versions have been built or ordered to date. But the BK 117 continues to be used as a test-bed for a variety of upgraded systems, including a recently exhibited all-composite airframe version.

MESSERSCHMITT-BOLKOW-BLOHM/ KAWASAKI BK 117

Main rotor diameter:	36 ft., 1 in.
Tail rotor diameter:	6 ft., 5 in.
Length:	32 ft., 6.25 in.
Width:	5 ft., 3 in.
Height:	11 ft., .25 in.
Weight (maximum take-off):	7,055 lbs.
Cruising speed:	158 mph
Maximum altitude:	15,000 ft.
Range:	363 miles
Date of first flight:	1979

AGUSTA A 109A MARK II

Agusta of Italy has been manufacturing helicopters since 1952, when the company was first licensed to produce the Bell 47. Since then, Agusta has produced a variety of helicopters using designs from Bell, Boeing, and Sikorsky. The A 109 series, however, is Agusta's own design and has established itself as one of the premier helicopters in the light multirole class. The A 109 first flew in 1971 and is now manufactured in a variety of models, including civilian, general military, forward observation, and a "high and hot" (high operating altitude and hot climate temperature) export version.

Conventional in its overall design, the A 109 is a high-speed, high-performance helicopter that can fulfill a variety of light helicopter missions. Except for the "high and hot" A 109K version, all A 109 aircraft share the same basic engines, two Allison 250-C20B turboshafts that produce 400 horsepower. The helicopter features a fully articulated four-bladed single main rotor. Retractable tricycle landing gear creates an aerodynamically "clean" aircraft that enables it to cruise at speeds of up to 178 miles per hour. The basic A 109A Mark II is made of light metal alloys and is constructed in four main sections that are joined together.

In its standard configuration, the A 109 carries a crew of two and up to six passengers. In the VIP mode, the layout reduces seating to four or five and adds such amenities as wet bar and sound system. Currently, civilian versions are used for water dropping for fire fighters, executive VIP transportation, medical life-flights, news reporting, law enforcement, and cargo hauling. Depending on the aircraft's mission, additional equipment can include external cargo sling, a rescue hoist, water bomber container, stretcher carriers, and a host of specialized interior packages.

The military version of the aircraft features many of the same attributes as the civilian version. Most military versions also include complete dual instrumentation and controls, sliding doors, armored seats for the crew, main rotor and tail rotor brake, high-load cargo floor, and external supports for outside cargo lift.

Above: The Agusta 109, Italy's first multirole light helicopter, has been purchased by a number of military and civilian organizations around the world. **Left:** The 109's retractable landing gear and flush, riveted skin make for a graceful aerodynamic design.

Depending upon the mission, the military version of the A 109A Mark II helicopter can be configured several ways. The "Aerial Scout" version can be armed with a variety of weaponry and pressed into service as a fast and agile reconnaissance aircraft. The "Light Attack Armor" version is designed to go after tanks, armored columns, and other hard targets with antitank weaponry that includes the TOW and Mathogo missiles. In the "Light Attack" role, the aircraft carries a combination of machine guns, remote gun pods, and various rocket launchers. The "Command and Control" model can also be armed with rockets and machine guns but is usually lightly armed. This model is used for target designation and directing other helicopters in the battlefield attack. The "Utility/Emergency Medical Service"

helicopter can be configured to carry up to seven combat soldiers or up to two stretcher patients with medical assistance personnel. This version can also support a rescue hoist and a cargo hook for external loads. The "Mirach" version carries two Mirach 100 Remote Piloted Vehicles that can be used for battlefield surveillance, reconnaissance, targeting, electronic countermeasures, direct attack targeting, and decoying enemy fire. The "ECM" model is the electronic countermeasures and electronic warfare version. It hosts the latest in sophisticated avionics and electronic systems, chaff dispensers in the tail section, and weapons dictated by mission needs.

In the naval model, the helicopter will usually feature a nonretractable landing gear, additional radars, automatic navigation system, tie-down/

anchorage points for deck securing, and additional fuel tank capacity. The naval model is used for antiship missions, electronic warfare, standoff missile guidance, antisubmarine warfare patrol, over-the-horizon reconnaissance, and search and rescue operations. In this version, the helicopter can be armed with antiship missiles, antisubmarine torpedoes, sonobuoys, and air-to-air antiaircraft missiles.

Two additional versions of the A 109 are also offered and remain in production. The A 109 EOA is currently being procured by the Italian Army as a new advanced observation helicopter. The lengthened nose can accommodate additional avionics and sensor packages. The EOA version also has up-rated engines for better "high and hot" performance, crash-survival fuel tanks, slid-

ing main cabin doors, and a wide variety of armament options.

The Agusta A 109K, developed as the "high and hot" variant, was built and designed specifically for the marketplaces of the Middle East and Africa. Major differences include up-rated Turbomeca Arriel IK turboshaft engines producing 722 horsepower, an up-rated transmission, new composite hub rotor design, composite blades with a hardened surface that resists chipping and damage caused by sand, redesigned nonretractable landing gear, and a variety of selected weaponry.

The A 109 continues to be one of the Agusta's most successful designs. With the wide variety of models offered for civilian and military use, and sales that have already topped 300 aircraft, the A 109 will be around for a long time.

Opposite, top: *The Agusta 109 was designed originally as a civilian helicopter.*
Opposite, bottom: *The 109's versatility and ability to carry a wide range of armaments have made it a successful military helicopter.*
Above: *The military version of the Agusta 109 includes dual controls, armored seats, flotation bags, and infrared suppressors on the engine exhausts.*

AGUSTA A 109A MARK II

Main rotor diameter:	36 ft., 1 in.
Tail rotor diameter:	6 ft., 8 in.
Length:	35 ft., 1.5 in.
Width:	4 ft., 8 in.
Height:	10 ft., 10 in.
Weight (maximum take-off):	5,732 lbs.
Cruising speed:	178 mph
Maximum altitude:	18,000 ft.
Range:	368 miles
Date of first flight:	1971

The Agusta 109 can be armed with a pivoted 7.62mm or .50 caliber machine gun and two rocket launcher stations.

AGUSTA 129 MONGOOSE

In 1972, the Italian Army published requirements for a light helicopter to perform in an antitank role. The Agusta 129 Mongoose met or exceeded the required characteristics. The Agusta 129 is the only European attack helicopter flying to date. The aircraft is a multirole helicopter that carries an amazing range of weaponry and is capable of flying in any weather or at night.

The Agusta 129 is a twin-engine, four-bladed attack helicopter, built largely of composite materials. Two Rolls Royce GEM 2 Mark 1004 engines, each producing 895 horsepower, power the helicopter. Vents in the engine exhausts mix cold air with the hot exhaust for infrared suppression. The engines are controlled by digital electronic controls, are simple in design, and can be changed under field conditions in 30 minutes. The engines drive the transmission directly at 27,500 revolutions per minute, eliminating the need for a reduction gear and increasing the helicopter's survivability. The transmission can operate for 30 minutes after loss of lubrication.

The main rotor (Agusta-designed and patented) is four-bladed; each blade is mounted on a single elastomeric (synthetic rubber or plastic) bearing. The blades themselves are made of NOMEX with leading edge strips of steel-titanium, and the blade tips are designed to produce a low-noise profile. The main rotor blades can withstand hits from .50 caliber or 23 millimeter weapons and can cut branches up to five inches thick. The NOMEX blades can also withstand the severe abrasion from trees, power lines, and other material occasioned when flying close to the ground.

Tandem seating for the pilot and weapons operator provides excellent visibility in all directions. The pilot sits behind and above the weapons operator, and both are surrounded by armored panels and protected by Martin-Baker armored seats. The helicopter has been designed for crash survivability based on United States Department of Defense military standards. In the event of a violent impact, the cabin will not be crushed by more than 20 percent of its volume, and the Martin-Baker seats will reduce an impact of 43-G force to an impact of 15 G's or less. The airframe contains

The Agusta 129 Mongoose is an Italian designed and built helicopter.

AGUSTA 129 MONGOOSE

Main rotor diameter:	39 ft., .6 in.
Tail rotor diameter:	7 ft., 4.25 in.
Length:	40 ft., 3 in.
Width:	11 ft., 9.6 in.
Height:	10 ft., 10.5 in.
Weight (maximum take-off):	9,039 lbs.
Cruising speed:	161 mph
Maximum altitude:	7,840 ft.
Range:	390 miles
Date of first flight:	1983

Above: *The Mongoose's pilot and weapons operator are protected by armored seats and panels.* **Opposite, top:** *The Agusta 129 Mongoose is a potent antitank weapon on NATO's southern flank.* **Opposite, bottom:** *This Mongoose is equipped with TOW missiles and 2.75-inch free-flight rockets.*

roll bars, and the main rotor is well supported. The fuel tanks are self-sealing, and the fixed tricycle landing gear can survive an impact of 32.8 feet per second.

To protect against ballistic damage, all flight control linkages are protected within the rotary mast, which also ensures against icing and reduces radar reflectivity. Provision has been made for a mast-mounted sight that can be used for aiming rockets, machine guns, or lasers while on attack or scout missions.

The Mongoose has two separate fuel systems with cross-feeds to each self-sealing tank, three hydraulic servocontrol systems (one a backup for the tail rotor), and a backup fly-by-wire for the main and tail rotors. Should everything fail at the same time, the pilot can still control the aircraft through a mechanical foot pedal system.

The Harris Corporation's Government Information Systems Division of Melbourne, Florida, has developed a fully Integrated Multiplex System based on two redundant interfaced computers.

The computers manage the helicopter's electronics and flight controls by dividing them into seven basic subsystems and then displaying to the pilot and weapons operator only the data needed. This data includes communication, navigation, autopilot, fly-by-wire, engine performance, transmission and hydraulic systems conditions, fuel, electrical, aircraft performance, cautions and warnings, sight and Pilot Night Vision, and fire control, not including TOW missiles.

The pilot and weapons operator are as well equipped for combat as state-of-the-art technology can provide. The Mongoose uses Honeywell's Night Vision System, which uses Forward Looking Infra Red with a display for both pilot and weapons operator. Both pilot and weapons operator wear the Honeywell Integrated Helmet Display and Sight System. The Mongoose can be configured for a number of other roles (scouting, naval tasks, or tactical transport) as well as air-to-air combat when fitted with either the French Mistral or the United States Stinger missile systems.

Glossary

Air-to-air missile: Weapon (such as a Sidewinder missile) launched from one flying aircraft against another flying aircraft.

Air-to-ground missile: Weapon (such as a *TOW* rocket) launched from an aircraft against ground positions such as troop convoys, tanks, or armored personnel carriers.

Air-to-sea missile: Weapon (such as a Mark 46 torpedo) launched from an aircraft against enemy ships or submarines.

Angle of attack: The angle, or "pitch," at which the *leading edge* of a blade meets the airstream.

Antisubmarine warfare (ASW): The search, detection, and attack against enemy submarines. Helicopters often perform all roles using sophisticated equipment, but ships or attack planes may also be called in to assist.

Autorotate: The ability of a helicopter to descend at a controlled rate by allowing its *main rotors* to spin freely should the engine break down.

Avionics: The various electrical devices and systems in a helicopter that aid in flying, weapons operation, and navigation.

Chaff: Streamers of aluminum dropped by an aircraft to create false images on enemy radar.

Collective pitch: The lever in the cockpit that controls the *angle of attack* of the rotor blades as a unit. The steeper the pitch is, the more *lift* that is generated. The collective pitch controls vertical ascent and descent.

Cowling: The removable covering for the helicopter's engine and, sometimes, parts of the *fuselage* also.

Cyclic pitch: The lever in the cockpit that controls the direction a helicopter travels by tilting the *main rotor* blades in that direction. The cyclic pitch controls the horizontal direction of the helicopter.

Elastomer: A synthetic material used to manufacture the hinges that connect a helicopter blade to the hub. Since the material is made in one piece and can flex and bend, it is far simpler, requires lower maintenance, and withstands stress better than metal.

American AH-1S HueyCobra.

Fairing: The skin covering that smoothes the outline of the *fuselage,* thus reducing air drag.

Fléchette: A very small arrow-shaped round of ammunition. They are commonly used in large clusters against enemy personnel. Fléchettes can be contained in rockets, artillery rounds, or specially designed bullets. After the round is fired, the covering that holds the fléchettes in a compact mass strips away, and the individual fléchettes continue toward the target, diverging slightly from one another. The fléchettes from a single rocket round fired from a helicopter can blanket an area of several hundred square feet.

Fuselage: The main body of a helicopter that accommodates crew, passengers, and cargo.

Head-up display: A vision plate in front of the pilot that displays all the flight control information needed by the pilot to fly his craft. The information, presented in simplified and symbolic form, appears within the wearer's line of vision so that he need only refocus his eyes to read the data. This enables the pilot to keep control of the aircraft without having to turn his head or shift his vision from outside the cockpit to within.

Honeycomb: Metal or plastic expanded into a thick mesh and bonded between covering sheets. The cross section of the mesh between the covering produces a rigid but lightweight skin covering.

Horsepower-to-weight ratio: Engine horsepower delivered per pound of helicopter.

Landing zone: A designated space in which a helicopter can land and usually associated with combat operations.

Leading edge: The "front" of the rotor blade. It is the edge of the blade that leads the rest of the blade through the airstream. Compare *trailing edge.*

Lift: The upward push resulting from air flowing over a surface that is curved on the top but flat on the bottom. The air flowing across the top has farther to travel and therefore is less dense than the air below the wing.

Main rotor: The helicopter's "wing," containing the blades that provide *lift.* The main rotor can have as few as two blades or as many as seven or eight.

Medevac: Medical evacuation of injured personnel by helicopter from a battlefield.

Monocoque: A light metal structure over which metal skin is stretched. The metal skin carries a large part of the structural stress.

NATO: North Atlantic Treaty Organization, a military alliance of Western European powers with the United States.

No tail rotor (NOTAR): Elimination of the *tail rotor* in favor of compressed air emitted through the tail boom to counteract *main rotor torque.*

Over-the-horizon: Amphibious forces assault technique. Helicopters ferry the assault force and its equipment to secure the beach. The helicopters depart from surface ships out of range—over-the-horizon—of enemy guided missiles.

Payload: The weight in cargo, personnel, or weapons that a helicopter is able to carry under its own power.

American AH-1S HueyCobra.

Pintle: A pin, bolt, or hook to which a gun is attached, giving the gun the ability to turn.

Pitch arm: That part of the *rotor hub* attached to the *root* and rotor blade that controls the blade's *angle of attack.*

Pod: A protective compartment on the *fuselage* of a helicopter that contains fuel, radar equipment, weapons, and other accoutrements of helicopter flight.

Root: The part of the *rotor hub* that attaches the blades to the hub.

Rotor hub: The assembly that turns the *main rotor.* It is composed of various elements, such as the drive shaft, *swash plates,* hinges, *roots, pitch arms,* etc.

Search and rescue: The process of searching for a downed aircraft pilot in enemy territory and airlifting him back to friendly territory.

Side-by-side: Helicopter seating arrangement in which the cockpit crew members sit beside one another.

Sponson: Structure or platform that projects from the side of a helicopter and holds a gun.

Stabilizer: The horizontal section or wing at the end of the tail boom that helps the helicopter remain stable while in flight.

Swash plate: Plates or fixtures atop the *main rotor* mast. The lower swash plate is fixed to the mast but can tilt in any direction when actuated by hydraulic rods linked to the cyclic control. The upper swash plate rotates on the lower swash plate and moves with it. They are used to control the direction of horizontal flight.

Tail rotor: A small set of blades at the end of the tail boom that counters the action of *torque.*

Tandem: Helicopter seating arrangement in which the cockpit crew members sit one behind the other.

Torque: The force produced by the *main rotor* of a helicopter that causes the aircraft to turn or twist in the opposite direction of the main rotor blades. Torque must be countered for the helicopter to fly with any control. Various methods have been applied through the years. The two most common methods are counterrotating main rotor blades or using a small *tail rotor* that pushes in the opposite direction of torque.

TOW (Tube-launched, Optically tracked, Wire-guided): Missile used primarily as a antitank weapon. TOW can be launched from ground or airborne vehicles.

Trailing edge: The "back" edge of the main rotor blade. The part of the blade that follows the rest of the blade as it moves through the airstream. Compare *leading edge.*

Warsaw Pact: Military alliance of Eastern European communist countries with the Soviet Union.

INDEX